RAPE IN PRISON

Publication Number 971
AMERICAN LECTURE SERIES®

A Publication in
The BANNERSTONE DIVISION of
AMERICAN LECTURES IN BEHAVIORAL SCIENCE
AND THE LAW

Editor
RALPH SLOVENKO, B.E., LL.B., M.A., Ph.D.
Wayne State University
Law School
Detroit, Michigan

Rape

In Prison

By

ANTHONY M. SCACCO, JR.,
B.S.S., Bs.Ed., M.A., Ed.D.

Educational Criminologist

*Formerly, Department of Corrections
State of Connecticut*

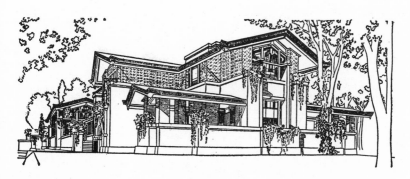

CHARLES C THOMAS • PUBLISHER

Springfield Illinois U.S.A.

HV
8836
.S3

Published and Distributed Throughout the World by
CHARLES C THOMAS • PUBLISHER
Bannerstone House
301-327 East Lawrence Avenue, Springfield, Illinois, U.S.A.

© 1975, by CHARLES C THOMAS • PUBLISHER
ISBN 0-398-03314-5
Library of Congress Catalog Card Number: 74-13818

Library of Congress Cataloging in Publication Data

Scacco, Anthony M.
  Rape in Prison.

  (American lecture series, publication no. 971. A publication in the
Bannerstone division of American lectures in behavioral science and the
law)
  Bibliography: p.
  1. Prisoners—Sexual behavior. I. Title.
[DNLM: 1. Prisons. 2. Rape. 3. Sex deviation. HV8836 S277r]
HV8836.S3   365'.6   74-13818
ISBN 0-398-03314-5

Printed in the United States of America
M-3

To My Parents
who also await the fulfillment
of my dream
and
To Gerald Hansen
whose encouragement made it
all possible

FOREWORD

R APE, BOTH HETEROSEXUAL and homosexual, has traditionally been discussed in terms of either individual
psychopathology or situational anomaly. Homosexual activity in prison has been attributed to the failure of prison
authorities to properly identify and segregate overt and latent
homosexuals from the general population and to the prag-
matic approach to the sexual needs of heterosexuals confined
in a monosexual institution for long periods of time.

We have long known however that sex, both among animals and humans, has been used either to establish, or as a
symbol of, the dominant-submissive relationship—and as an
expression of either group or individual hostility.

Dr. Scacco in this interesting study of one aspect of the
prison sex problem has identified an important facet of sexual aggression: Rape as an expression of ethnic hostility and
as a tactic in the ethnic power struggle which in the past
decade has become a major fact of life in the penal institutions of many of our states.

Where Dr. Scacco has broken new ground is in his discussion of the use of coerced sexual submission in the newly
politicized prison community—and particularly in his discussion of black rape of white inmates as punishment and
debasement.

There will be much criticism of Dr. Scacco's approach—
we are a nation of ostriches and we are overly-sensitive
(quite rightly when you consider our history) of anything
which, masquerading as science, smacks of racism. I do not
think such attacks can be honestly or logically directed
against this study. From my own experience and studies, I
know that much of what Dr. Scacco states is true—and I have
discussed this racial-sexual phenomenon with so many perpe-

trators and victims as to convince me that both his analysis and his emphasis are fairly close to the mark.

This is an area which needs work. Both academic criminologists (and their colleagues in the behavioral sciences) and correctional administrators might well shed their puritanical vestments and cast aside their racial shibboleths and address themselves to an all-too-real problem of institutional survival which if unsolved will spew forth from our prisons an ever increasing number of severly traumatized victims.

DONAL E. J. MACNAMARA
Professor Of Correction Administration
John Jay College of Criminal Justice
City University of New York

ACKNOWLEDGMENTS

I WOULD LIKE TO acknowledge with gratitude the encouragement given me by Professor Ralph Slovenko of Wayne State University, for suggesting the treatment of such a subject at length. My thanks are also due to Michael Derison who took time from his own writing to make comments about my endeavor and to Professor Gene Fappiano of Southern Connecticut State College for listening to my many plans for the text. Mr. Raymond Coyle, Administrator of Institutions for the Department of Corrections, State of Connecticut cautioned the need for constructive criticism of such a topic and Siegfried Clemens' knowledge of where to find the facts was indispensible to me. Stuart J. Miller of Washington and Jefferson College encouraged me to "go on" and state what I found; the work of Professor Donal MacNamara of John Jay College of Criminal Justice and Professor Edward Sagarin of City College, made it easier to make my presentation. Dr. Mary Calderone, Executive Director of SIECUS whose work in the field of human sexuality is as important as Kinsey and Pomeroy, talked with me about the need for sex education in the field of Corrections and Dr. Derek Burleson of SIECUS, recommended sources for further exploration in this writing. Mary Freney who was more than a librarian but a personal friend throughout this endeavor. To Tom Santoro who helped bring this book to a meaningful conclusion.

CONTENTS

xi

RAPE IN PRISON

SEXUAL VICTIMIZATION, THE CULMINATION OF EXPLOITATION IN MALE CORRECTIONAL INSTITUTIONS

THE END RESULT of victimization in a correctional institution is usually sexual aggression and domination as a political act based on a show of force.[1] It is more than an act of sexual release as a result of heterosexual deprivation "since most prisoners do not seem to feel an overwhelming sexual need, male homosexuality (and aggression) in this context must be seen as something more complex than merely the outcome of sexual desire or the need for physical release." [2] It is an act whereby one male (or group of males) seeks testimony to what he considers is an outward validation of his masculinity.[3] This is not to understate the fact that tension [4] and the abnormal setting [5] of institutionalization do

---

[1] Peter C. Buffum, *Homosexuality in Prisons* (Washington, D.C., National Institute of Law Enforcement and Criminal Justice, U.S. Government Printing Office, February, 1972), p. 16.

[2] *Ibid.*, p. 14 (parenthesis mine).

[3] John H. Gagnon, and William Simon, "The Social Meaning Of Prison Homosexuality," *Federal Probation* (Washington D. C., Administrative Office of U.S. Courts in Cooperation with Bureau of Prisons of U.S. Department of Justice, Vol. 32, No. 1, 1968), p. 26; Buffum, *op. cit.*, p. 15.

[4] Harry L. Lyston, "Stress in Correctional Institutions," *Journal of Social Therapy* (New York, Official Publication of Medical Correctional Association, Vol. 6, 1960), pp. 216-224.

[5] Herbert A. Block, "Social Pressure of Confinement Toward Sexual Devia-

not add to the phenomenon of sexual assault; however, the aggressive inmates do not superimpose themselves on the dominated because they (dominant) are special or rare individuals. On the contrary, their behavior is apparently a learned pattern since the act of sexual dominance appears to be a cultural phenomena originating from the very fabric of the American social structure since "the source of this set of values (sexual behavior available to the inmates) does not reside in the prison experience, but outside in the community at large. Thus, the prison provides a situation to which prior sexual and social styles and motives must be adapted and shaped." [6] What the institution does, then, is merely to lend itself to attitudes that are already preformed, and embellish them somewhat because of the like attitudes and apparent needs of the inmate population, as well as the administrative and custodial staff.[7]

Therefore, the act of sexual aggression within correctional institutions is not, as the public may believe, a *sui generis* result of incarceration; it is not the act of homosexual perverts. Davis has pointed out that sexual assaults in the Philadelphia prison system can be classified as "epidemic" [8] leaving the rational man to conclude that even heterosexually-oriented males are partaking in this kind of conduct.

The head of one agency has offered what he considers the answer to the sexual attacks within penal institutions, and his observations are not without some truth. He stated that "such plays as *Fortune and Men's Eyes*, and most articles on homosexual rape in prisons are not homosexual at all, but heterosexuals, usually black men raping white boys for power and revenge. Homosexuals do not have to force another person to have sex with them in or out of prison; we have all the sex we can get. If prisons and their guards and inmates will

---

tion," *Journal of Social Therapy* (New York, Official Publication of Medical Correctional Association, Vol. 1, 1955), pp. 112-125.

    [6] Buffum, *op. cit.,* p. 9 (parenthesis mine).

    [7] See Chapter 2 of this volume concerning staff's role in aggression.

    [8] Alan J. Davis, "Sexual Assaults In The Philadelphia Prison System and Sheriffs' Vans," *Trans-Action* (New Brunswick New Jersey, Rutgers University, Vol. 6, No. 2, December, 1968), p. 9.

use common sense . . . they will get rid of most of the sex problems. Also, it is not possible to turn someone homosexual even under such circumstances . . . people will have the same sex problems in or out of prisons. If prison guards do their duty and keep the peace, there will be no rapes." [9]

Whether or not the black inmate population outnumbers that of the whites on any given day in penal institutions, personal experience, as well as that of other research [10] in the field of sexual aggression in prison, bears out the fact that there is a definite reversal of majority and minority roles once within the walls. More frankly speaking, blacks appear to be taking out their frustrations and feelings of exploitation on the other inmates in the form of sexual attack and domination, as "the oppressive characteristics of race relations in the society as a whole penetrate the relationships between whites and Negroes inside the prisons." [11] Yet, in spite of all that is happening, it is still quite true that "we who work in prisons (jails, training school and reformatories) undoubtedly have less understanding of the phenomena of sex in the closed communities in which we operate than in any other single problem we face each working day." [12]

In the final analysis the correctional system cannot be blamed for causing the behavior within the walls for, as Tannenbaum poetically put it a long time ago, "the community provides the attitudes, the point of view, the philosophy of life, the example, the motives, the contacts, the friendships and the incentives. No child brings those into the world. He finds them there and available for use and elaboration. The community gives the criminal his materials and habits as it

---

[9] Personal communication, William Glover, Homosexual Information Center, Los Angeles, California, March 2, 1970.

[10] Stuart J. Miller and Clemens Bartollas, "The White Victim In A Black Society." Unpublished paper presented at the Annual Meeting Of The American Society Of Criminology, New York, November 2-6, 1973; Davis, *op. cit.*, p. 15.

[11] Buffum, *op. cit.*, p. 22.

[12] Arthur V. Huffman, "Sex Deprivation In A Prison Community," *Journal of Social Therapy* (New York, Official Publication of Medical Correctional Association, Vol. 6, No. 1-4, 1960), p. 171 (parenthesis mine); see also Chapter 4, *The Scapegoat Is Almost Always White*.

gives the doctor, the lawyer, and the teacher and the candlestick maker theirs." [13]

Precisely what then are correctional institutions and their staffs responsible for concerning sexual actions and aggression of the inmates entrusted to their care? Primarily, Corrections is required to inform the public about what actually happens behind the walls, who the victims of these attacks are, and where the responsibility for such action lies, even when the staff is at fault. Corrections must clean its own house and in many instances this is a difficult task, for some members in this occupation [14] add to the aggression already being practiced by many of the inmates on the weaker residents. This book addresses itself to these vital issues and offers alternatives that can help alleviate sexual aggression in the correctional setting, while leading to a better understanding of this phenomena in its general context.

---

[13] Frank Tannenbaum, "The Professional Criminal," *The Century,* 110:577 (May-October, 1925).

[14] See Chapter 2 of this volume.

CHAPTER **2**

INSTITUTIONAL SETTING

While society in the United States gives the example of the most extended liberty, the prisons of the same country offer a spectacle of the most complete despotism.
De Tocqueville, 1830

THERE ARE THOSE authors who refer to our present day correctional institutions as "cloacal regions";[1] for in "twenty-three states our prisons are from seventy to one-hundred and ten years old and should have been torn down long ago and replaced by another type of institution."[2] The sad fact is that they have not been torn down, nor are they viewed realistically by contemporary society for what they really are, which is "little more than places to keep people— warehouses of human degradation."[3] In reality conditions such as overcrowding, aggression, and racism have made them infinitely worse since the era of their construction. In most instances our penal institutions stand as sentinels to a nineteenth century philosophy of punishment for the offender so that he will mend his evil ways.

From training schools for young offenders to maximum security prisons for adults, all penal institutions have one element in common, and that is the traumatic break between

---

[1] Peter C. Buffum, *Homosexuality In Prisons* (Washington, D.C., National Institute of Law Enforcement and Administration of Justice, U.S. Government Printing Office, February, 1972) p. 5.

[2] Kenyon J. Scudder, "The Open Institution," *Annals of American Academy of Political and Social Science*, 239:79 (May, 1954).

[3] Ramsey Clark, *Crime In America* (New York, Pocket Books, 1971), p. 193.

life as it is lived in free society and the manner in which it must be lived in confinement, for in fact:

> On the outside, the individual can hold objects of self-feeling, such as his body, his immediate actions, his thoughts, and some of his possessions, clear of contact with alien and contaminating things. But, in the total institution, these territories of self are violated, the boundary that the individual places between his being and the environment is invaded and the embodiment of self profaned." [4]

In reality, the only individuality allowed is that which is taken, usually in the form of a violation of the rule. So it is with sexual aggression; the dominant ones invade the actual physical being of their victim and take what they want. The institutional setting itself allows this aggression, for by its very nature and structure it is conducive to attack. Attack can and frequently does go unnoticed, either with the help of other inmates acting as sentinels, or worse, because guards are overworked, purposefully inattentive, or even more tragic, the officers may be part of the syndrome of sexual aggression and exploitation itself, in both an overt and covert way.

Juvenile institutions are usually overlooked in studies concerning incarceration, or little analysis of the conditions within these institutions is undertaken in favor of the larger and more secure settings of the prison. Yet, it is precisely on the level of the young juvenile and adult that institutionalization takes its physical and psychological toll. The morbid physical settings of our correctional institutions are the "homes for some 100,000 children sitting in jail-like institutions throughout the country. They are as young as six, most perhaps . . . are not delinquent. They have committed no criminal actions. They are in trouble with their schools or victims of bad homes or no homes, or perhaps runaways, or emotionally disturbed, or mentally retarded or neurologically impaired." [5]

---

[4] Erving Goffman, *Asylums* (New York, Anchor Books; Doubleday and Company, 1961), p. 23.

[5] Charles Mangel, "How To Make A Criminal Out Of a Child," *Look*, 35:3 (June 29, 1971).

It is an established fact that the older inmates are educated in the ways of aggression as a result of the training they receive as inmates of youth institutions; training from the sub-culture [6] is carried with them as they continue their life of incarceration in jails, reformatories, and eventually to prison itself. Over 80 percent of serious crimes committed in the nation are perpetrated by ex-inmates who find themselves returned to prison for new crimes or for parole violation.

In most instances the young offender receives his initiation into a loss of his privacy the very first day he enters the training school as a result of his entry into the reception and orientation process itself. Upon his entrance into the institution, the young inmate must undergo a physical examination for venereal disease, a standard procedure followed in all penal institutions. Here, as in jail, the nurse is usually entrusted with the examination of incoming boys. When registered nurses are not available, and this is frequently the situation, the examination is conducted by a trustee trained at the institution. It is here that sexual exploitation usually begins. Naturally, the inmate must strip for the exam. Other trustees usually make sure that they are present with some excuse of doing some assigned job around the hospital area. They also unofficially examine the new inmate and pass their opinion of the inmate's body and sex organ around the institution to those who might be interested in such information. Even without his knowledge, the new inmate has already had his privacy invaded by more than the nurse; in reality he has presented his body to the entire inmate population for scrutiny.

The inmate is then sent to the psychologist who administers the usual tests considered relevant for psychological evaluation of offenders. Most of the boys treat the whole procedure as a charade and tell the examiner what they believe he wants to hear rather than what they really see in the test

---

[6] Stanton Wheeler, "Socialization in Correctional Institutions," in *Crime and Justice*, Leon Radzinowicz and Marvin Wolfgang, eds. (New York, Basic Books, 1971). (section on Inmate Subculture), Vol. 3, Criminal in Confinement, pp. 97-115).

itself. Unfortunately, records are kept and even later in their careers, the same offenders must again submit to the same tests, only in these instances much depends on the way institutional committees judge these tests. Dr. Powleson, formerly resident psychiatrist at San Quentin, often attended Adult Authority hearings in which board members attempted to interpret Rorschach test results relative to parole decisions. "It is very hard for even a skilled person to interpret these tests," he said. "To use them to predict behavior is about as valid as using a crystal ball." [7] Yet, untrained individuals were often responsible for attempting to interpret such sophisticated tests and extending the time a man had to serve in prison on their interpretation.

Having completed this phase of the orientation, the incoming inmate then visits his social worker who is responsible for placing him in the appropriate cottage. The social worker has a complete file on the offender, from the time of his birth up to and including the trial and sentence he has received. These files should be much more help toward rehabilitation than they are. Unfortunately, and in most instances, the profile that is presented in this report is taken and superimposed on the youth that is sentenced. Should he be labeled as a "bad-ass" by his local police department and be considered a troublemaker by a teacher or the principal at his high school, then this is the opinion and reputation that will be stamped on him as he begins his stay at the institution.

Likewise, should the newcomer be labeled as a weak boy (exploitable) or known to have engaged in homosexual activity on the outside, then this information most assuredly becomes known, not only to the treatment and custodial staff, but also to the inmate population itself. Already the new inmate has a major strike against him and is being sexually exploited without his knowledge; the staff more often than not makes his homosexual behavior known to the other in-

---

[7] Jessica Mitford, *Kind and Unusual Punishment* (New York, Alfred A. Knopf, 1971), p. 102.

mates, therefore establishing his reputation as a "punk", even before he enters his assigned cottage.

It is obvious that it is not the official orientation into the institution that is the most important reception given the new inmate, for what does not appear in the folder of the social worker, psychologist, and the doctor, is the unofficial, and most often more important, evaluation that the new-comer will receive from the other inmates and staff. As has been pointed out, this unofficial opinion has been colored to a large degree, not only by the actions and mannerisms of the boy himself, but also by the reports and institutional gossip of the professional staff that most assuredly precedes the inmate to his cottage. In some instances the staff adds to sexual exploitation by referring to the new inmate with such tags as "freak," "sissy," and "girl." [8] The language and what it connotes is picked up by the other young inmates and serves as a vehicle to the physical acts of sexual exploitation to which the new inmate is later subjected. In maximum security institutions for adults, this type of baiting by the custodial staff is done purposefully to aid in the sexual exploitation of the inmate being so labeled. This is a way in which the staff can directly influence the exploitation of an inmate they do not like or wish to see abused.

Jail Within a Jail—No Place to Run

All training schools and detention centers have their maximum security units where extremely troublesome, angry, frustrated, or sometimes dangerous boys find themselves confined and often sexually exploited. Connecticut School for Boys referred to its lock-up area as the "treatment unit." It was a group of solitary confinement cells set apart from the rest of the institution on a maximum security basis. Here the more difficult boys were supposed to receive special attention and treatment by the school psychiatrist and other members of the professional and clinical staff. However, the

---

[8] Alan J. Davis, "Sexual Assaults in the Philadelphia Prison System and Sheriff's Vans," *Trans-Action*, 6:13 (December, 1968).

boys spent most of the time sleeping and reading materials brought in to keep them quiet.

Sexual exploitation was possible in this special security section because it was filled to overflowing most of the time. The state law is that each boy was to be locked up on an individual basis. In reality, however, two occupants were often housed together in one cell. Sexual experimentation as well as exploitation took place under these circumstances; locked in a 5′ x 8′ cell with a metal door (with just a slot for visitors and custodians to peer through and opened only from the outside), an unwilling boy had no choice but to submit to the desires of the inmate with whom he was confined.

Charles Mangel, *Look's* senior editor, was shocked to find such lock-up situations as these in Illinois and other states. He found youngsters fourteen years of age and younger locked in solitary confinement in a cell 5′x 10′ for seventy-one days. Also, he discovered that many inmates were controlled by the *cage men* who forcefully injected them with Thorazine®, one of the most potent tranquilizers known to modern science.[9]

At the training school, much of the exploitation occurred in the cottages themselves. Built nearly a century ago, these large mansion-like houses provided cellars, clothes rooms, little used hallways, and abandoned attics that were used by the dominant inmates for sexual assaults. Added to this is the fact that sleeping, showering and recreation are all group activities wherein a young resident hardly has any means of protecting his body should an individual or a group desire to exploit it.

It is a lugubrious note that the guards were screened off in a cage-like enclosure from the inmates while they were sleeping. Thus, guards were safe from inmates, while the inmates themselves were caged together with no protection from one another. There were many sexual assaults carried out during the night. Institutional records show more than one instance where a guard was caught sound asleep while on duty and could not even be aroused by the superintendent

[9] Mangel, *op. cit.*, p. 51.

after shaking him violently to awaken him. There is little chance that this type of security could prevent a weaker inmate from being exploited during the night.

Many sexual assaults were carried out in the clothes rooms located in each cottage. This area contained the bedding and daily work clothes used by the boys as well as some recreational gear. In spite of the strict ruling that anyone caught in the area would be subjected to solitary confinement, many a young resident was hauled off by one, two and even more stronger inmates, had a rag stuffed in his mouth, and was repeatedly raped.

The bathroom located within the main school building was practically termed a *combat zone* by the teachers and even the janitor of the building. Since all the boys from the cottages eventually made their way to the school building each day, it was a potential bombshell for tension and exploitation. Aggressors from each cottage often used the school as a common meeting ground to prove their prowess and power over inmates that they would not normally have access to, since each group was supposed to confine itself to its own cottage except for officially designated group meetings and school activities.

There were two official breaks during the morning and afternoon school sessions. During these rest periods the boys were supposed to go to the bathroom, get a drink of water, and return to class. The bathroom was the center ring for forced acts of sexual aggression. Most of the time the teacher and the janitor took turns standing within the bathroom and policing the five stand up urinals and the bathroom stalls, whose four sided cabinets had long since been removed so as to allow observation of the inmates by the staff. This was an extra precaution because much of the forced sexual acts used to take place within the confines of these closed bathroom stalls. Even with all these precautions, many of the inmates were made to pay up for debts that they incurred or they were merely the victims of one or more boys. In most instances the other inmates acted as a cover either by engaging the teacher or janitor in some type of conversation, or overtly staging a disturbance that would necessitate the attention of either or both men. During this time the bathroom was left free to those exploiting their victims. Because of exploitative acts such as these, as well as other general and serious disturbances caused by gangs as well as individual inmates, the main school building was eventually closed up completely in favor of a plan wherein each cottage would have its own classrooms and school atmosphere. The hope was not only to assist each inmate in a better academic sense, but also to limit the exploitation that was happening to those who could not defend themselves in the larger school building.

Detention Centers

Detention centers fare far worse in most cases concerning sexual aggression and exploitation within their confines. Originally designed to house inmates for a day or two, many of them now retain their charges for several months. The more overt tragedy of this setting is that the youngster is bereft of real services or aid. In most instances he is in a state of limbo: waiting to go to court; waiting to find out if his parents will take him back if he is released to their custody, or tragically—just waiting for anything. Senator Birch Bayh has stated that this type of treatment is happening to children "presently being held in detention centers, training schools, and other correctional institutions (who) have never been charged with the equivalent of an adult crime. Children labeled as "incorrigible, neglected, truant runaways, and in need of supervision, have come before juvenile courts all across this country in need of attention and guidance, only to be institutionalized and isolated with little or no hope of ever receiving proper care, simply because it doesn't exist." [10] New York found that there has been an almost complete breakdown in any services for its adjudicated young offenders in this type of detention center. Further, they discovered that "racism, consciously or unconsciously pervades

---

[10] Address by Senator Birch Bayh to the National Council of Juvenile Court Judges, Washington, D.C., July 12, 1971.

the system" [11] and that conditions are so serious that "changes must be made before yet another generation of children is destroyed." [12]

The detention center is therefore a true revolving door with thousands passing through them in the course of a year. Those youngsters on their way to court, or simply just waiting, can and do take what they want in the way of sexual satisfaction from other male inmates. In some detention centers females as young as ten and as old as sixteen are housed in the same building as males. Much of the male-to-male sexual domination and exploitation is caused by stronger boys seeking to impress *their woman* confined in the same center.

Jail Setting

It is with this backround that many of those who begin their careers in delinquency in a training school or detention center later find themselves confined to a jail. They take with them all the bitterness connected with victim and aggressor and learn more about both in their new home. The jail itself has its own system of aggression and its own setting that adds to the exploitation of those too weak to defend themselves. The negative physical and psychological setting inherent in most jails serves as a drawback that many inmates find too overwhelming to fight and merely give in to, in order to survive.

Orientation in Jail

In jail the orientation begins with the inmate undergoing a physical examination, only here sexual exploitation is much more overt. The *jockers* and *wolves* have put in their orders for certain body types, and the trustees either in charge of the examination itself or the area of the examining room, pay back favors by alerting the aggressors to the various types that are being admitted to the jail.

---

[11] "Childrens Justice Called a Failure by Judicial Panel," New York *Times*, October 23, 1973, p. 1.

[12] *Ibid.*

The new inmate is made to shower and step directly in line for his examination. He is made to bend over and grab his ankles and in this position he is examined not only for venereal disease, but also by the officers in charge to determine if he is attempting to smuggle contraband into the institution by hiding it in his rectum. This part of the examination is often drawn out by the guards to humiliate the inmate and let him know who his keepers are and will be for the duration of his stay. This type of indoctrination is given to any person who is *booked* into the jail, i.e. charged with an offense wherein he can legally be confined, be it for one hour, or for a year or more. There is no psychologist or social worker for the incoming inmate to visit, so he is assigned to his cell right after his physical exam, provided that his finger prints and "mug-shot" (photograph) have already been taken.

In most of our jails at present, the cells are already overcrowded with two and even three men sharing a space that barely accommodates one individual. This situation will probably get much worse as many states seek to close some of their institutions as an austerity measure and to give the public the impression that there are less offenders for the existing facilities, but in reality the opposite is true. Therefore, the incoming inmate has no choice in the cell he is given and must take what is assigned to him.

Often the jock of a particular cell block will see to it that a young new inmate is placed in his cell with the specific intent of sexually exploiting him. He may have already set him up with the help of other inmates through a plan disguised as that of a friend helping a new arrival. He may tell the inmate to stay close to him since there are a lot of "queers around here," that will "take him" (rape him) if he is caught alone. The jock may even arrange a false threat to the new inmate by having several of his friends threaten the newcomer with gang rape, with the jock arriving just in time to save him from this ordeal. The jock then expects to be paid for his protection, and the payment is in the form of sexual services to be rendered by the new inmate. Because he fears gang rape, the newcomer usually will seek the protection of the jock so as not to open the way to his being exploited by the others in the jail. Under these conditions he may consent [13] to the demands of the aggressor. It is this type of relationship that leads many guards and administrators to look upon most sexual relationships as something that those who are engaged in them desire. In reality it may be what the threatened inmate has to accept as the far lesser of two horrible fates that await him.

Often a relationship called *lugging* develops in a penal institution as a result of an older inmate taking a youngster as his own. Whether it be for protection or for sexual reasons, the older male *adopts* the younger boy and, as a sign of his possession, gives the boy a cross and chain to wear around his neck. This symbol serves as notice to other jocks that the one wearing it is already taken and anyone attempting to assault the boy will eventually have to deal with the older prisoner whose property is clearly marked by the obvious symbol. Thus, in many instances there is a dual aggression occurring relative to sexual assault in penal institutions. A jock may merely see an available victim and seek to exploit him, or he may prefer to fight for a male already the property of another jock. The latter form of aggression is the most violent and can lead to a rebellion since the other inmates will take sides, not only with the respective victim being fought over, but also with his owner in such a show of force.

Coupled with the conditions being described is the almost unbelievable fact that "despite frequent and tragic stories of suicide, rape, and abuse of youth, the placement of juveniles in jail has not abated in recent years." [14] The fact is that between 200,000 and 300,000 children will be put in local jails during 1973.[15] Although such states as Massa-

---

[13] Davis, *op. cit.*, p. 9.

[14] Honorable Tom Railsback (R.-Rep./Ill.), "Juveniles In Jail," United States Congressional Record vol. 119, no. 141, September 25, 1973 (these are the observations of Dr. Rosmary C. Sarri of The National Assessment Of Juvenile Corrections of the University of Michigan), p. E.-6019.

[15] *Ibid.*

chusetts have made valiant efforts toward abolishing [16] larger
juvenile detention facilities, specialists point out that youngsters continue to be placed in jails with older men and criticism of this practice "has not produced any significant
change in the vast majority of states and there . . . is no
reason to be optimistic today about reductions in the jailing
of children." [17]

No Room—Pressure Cooker State of Living

One of the most horrendous aspects of a jail sentence is the
fact that not only are the young housed with the older offenders, but those awaiting trial share the same quarters as
convicted inmates. The latter individuals have little to lose
in seeking sexual gratification through assault, for they have
to serve their time anyway, or so they reason to themselves.
The quarters in which these men have to spend their time
and the general living conditions of most jails in the country
add directly to the behavior of the men confined within
their walls.

The Whalley Avenue Correctional Center (jail) at New
Haven, Connecticut is merely one example of the type of
physical plant currently housing* offenders in the state. This
institution received a great deal of attention during the
Panther Rally in May of 1969; there were serious questions
raised about its capability to handle huge crowds should a
riot situation develop, and mass arrests occurred as a result
of the May Day Rally. The jail can contain approximately
three hundred but has frequently been known to be filled
with nearly 450 under crowded conditions. There is neither
running water nor toilets in the cells, and men have to
bathe in four sinks in a common bathroom. Normal bathroom requirements for the inmates are met through the use of
"slop buckets," or white porcelain pots that the inmates squat
over to relieve themselves. These are emptied every morning

---

* A new correctional facility is under construction in New Haven and
should be completed in the next three years.

[16] "Massachusetts Reforms to Doom Youth Prisons," New York *Times*,
January 31, 1972, p. 1.

[17] Railsback, *op. cit.*, p. E.-6019.

before breakfast call. More than one officer has gotten the contents of these buckets thrown on them during a disturbance at this jail.

The recreation yard is a concrete rectangle some fifty feet in width and one hundred feet in length. This is the playground for some 450 men, accessible only in the warmer months, for winter cold and snow render it unusable. During any recreation period the yard is divided into three distinct groups: the blacks at the far end of the court, the Puerto Ricans in the middle and the whites at the end. There is rarely any integration during sports events being played in the yard. Since the men seek to strip to the waist during recreation, this period serves as a good occasion for those interested in certain body types to pick who they will seek out to satisfy them later during the evening or just before lock up. It is interesting to note that the East Wing of the jail was once at Sing Sing Prison but was declared obsolete, dismantled, loaded on a barge, and shipped to Connecticut, where it was reassembled and has been in use ever since. The cell doors still are incapable of being locked and the less aggressive inmates and trustees are usually placed in this section.

Mr. Raymond Coyle, the warden at New Haven, once related to me that his biggest job was "protecting the inmates from one another, every moment of the day and night." [18] Evidently he was aware of the aggression and brutality that existed among the confined men for there was a special lock-up unit where those found guilty of attacking another inmate were placed. However, the warden was careful to relate that catching an inmate in the act, or having others testify to an attack, was a rare occurrence; the victim would rather suffer his fate than tell the institutional authorities or seek their protection. This was the case since the vicim feared further abuse from the aggressor once he was released, or retaliation from the aggressor's friends within the jail itself.

In Philadelphia in the Holmesberg Prison, a unit of the Philadelphia city-county jail system, conditions are almost as

---

[18] Informal conversations with the Warden while the author was acting Educational Director at the Whalley Avenue Correctional Center, 1971.

bad as those described above. Inmates are crowded three to a cell in a structure built over seventy years ago. Roaches and rats proliferate throughout the institution, but the men do have, at the least, cold water and toilets in their cells. But the threat of violence looms over the institution at all times. One inmate summed up the mood of the jail when he said, "At night this place is a real jungle; that's when you really got to watch out to survive." [19] Survival is the key issue in a setting of overcrowding and archaic facilities such as these.

South Carolina shares an equally horrid reputation, even though it is said to have one of the most advanced prison systems in the nation. Its Fairfield County Jail houses prisoners in jails whose walls are constructed entirely of bars. Her sister state, North Carolina, appears to be far worse off, for it has been said that "somewhere in North Carolina's prison system a boy will be raped once, maybe three or four times in one night by different men. Somewhere behind the bars an effeminate young man too weak or too scared to fight back will be auctioned as a homosexual partner. The victim might be serving as little as thirty days for public drunkenness. He might be a high school student from a good home who stole a car. He might be a businessman who was a solid citizen until he stole some money in one moment of desperation." [20] This type of intimidation appears to be quite common; Michigan's Wayne County Jail has candidly reported that "guards are unable to prevent cases of robbery, assault, and homosexual rape among inmates." [21]

On the West Coast conditions appear to be as serious. Men incarcerated in the Santa Cruz County Jail in California are kept in tiger cages with bars on top as well as the sides of each cell; conditions include "inadequate lighting, overcrowding, insufficient medical attention, and lack of protec-

---

[19] Herbert Kupferberg and Sid Ross, "A Waste Of Lives—And Your Money: The Shame of Our County Jails," *Parade* (November 4, 1973), p. 12.

[20] "Sexual Assaults and Forced Homosexual Relationships in Prison: Cruel and Unusual Punishment," *Albany Law Journal*, 36:433, 1972.

[21] Kupferberg and Ross, *op. cit.*, p. 14.

tion against beatings and homosexual attacks by other prisoners." [22]

In New York's Manhattan House of Detention, more notoriously known as the Tombs, "a desperate place of rats, beatings and murders," [23] conditions equalling and in most instances far surpassing those just described are the normal events each day for those who are confined within its walls. Much of it can be blamed on the lack of adequate facilities, overcrowding, racism and brutality on the part of some inmates and correctional personnel. Most of the men spend two-thirds of their time locked in a 6′ x 6′ x 9′ cell. Federal Judge Morris E. Lasker stated that "three years have passed since the Tombs' disturbance (and) the dismal conditions which still exist in the institution manifestly violate the Constitution and would shock the conscience of any citizen who knew them." [24]

It is of further significance to note that out of every one hundred inmates in the Tombs, sixty are black, twenty-seven Puerto Rican, and thirteen are white. When exploitation does occur, the figures should speak for themselves as to who the victim is and who the aggressor is. This facility is for men awaiting trial, and yet they have to bear ignominies far worse than any sentenced man has to endure. One inmate has been awaiting trial in the Tombs for nearly three years under these conditions.[25]

Overcrowding in the Tombs seems to be an institutional hazard. The official capacity is 932, but in 1970 it had more than 1,400 inmates, with three and sometime four prisoners assigned to a cell. An inmate can see his visitors by peering through a bullet proof plate glass window, and physical contacts are strictly forbidden for fear of weapons being smuggled into the jail. Thus, these men see their families through

---

[22] *Ibid.*

[23] James Mills, "I Have Nothing to Do With Justice, *Life,* 70:63, (March 12, 1972).

[24] Ted Morgan, "Entombed," *New York Times* Magazine Section, February 17, 1974, p. 14.

[25] *Ibid.*

an opening 6 x 16 inches and talk to their relatives over a
phone that is usually not in working order. Dr. Karl Menninger, after visiting the Tombs, said that this separation of
visitor from inmate is "like dangling a piece of raw meat in
front of a dog." [26] Even visitation privileges are limited since
they include only the immediate family, usually those only
sixteen and older (therefore children are barred from visiting) and the attorney representing the accused. It appears
that the comment made by Charles Dickens in 1842, after
visiting the original Tombs, can be safely repeated today. He
said, "What! Do you thrust your common offenders of the
police discipline of the town in such holes as these?" [27] Evidently we still do!

Many cases could be cited of actual rape of an individual in
jail,[28] but one in particular is chosen to let the reader hear the
events from an ordinary citizen. He is married with a family,
no previous criminal record, and a former Georgia legislator
and businessman who found himself the victim of a jail situation. William Laite was indicted and convicted in Texas of
perjury relating to a contract he had with the Federal Administration Housing Authority. He was sentenced to the
Tarrant County Jail in Fort Worth, Texas. The moment he
entered the *tank* or *day* room, he was approached by five men.
The first comment from one of them was, "I wonder if he
has any guts. We'll find out tonight, won't we? Reckon what
her name is; she looks ready for about six or eight inches.
You figure she will make us fight for it, or is she going to give
it to us nice and sweet like a good little girl? Naw, we'll have
to work her over first, but hell, that's half the fun, isn't it?" "I
couldn't move," said Laite. "I was terrified. This couldn't be
real. This couldn't be happening to me." [29] Laite was saved
from sexual assault because a seventeen-year-old youth was

[26] *Ibid.*, p. 24.

[27] American Friends Service Committee, *Struggle For Justice, A Report On Crime and Punishment In America* (New York, Hill and Wang, 1971), p. 8.

[28] Davis, *op. cit.*, pp. 9, 10, 12 for a vivid description of rape in jail and prison.

[29] William Laite, *The United States vs William Laite* (Washington, D.C., Acropolis Books, 1972), p. 42.

admitted to the day room as he was about to become the victim of the five men in the tank. The men saw the boy and turned on him, knocked him out, and then, "they were on him at once like jackals, ripping the coveralls off his limp body. Then as I watched in frozen fascination and horror, they sexually assaulted him, savagely and brutally like starving animals after a raw piece of meat. Then I knew what they meant about giving me six or eight inches." [30]

The attack did not end there according to Laite, for while the boy was still unconscious, the attackers jabbed his arms, neck and body with the burning tips of erasers of pencils, so that the boy's body twitched making it more sexually exciting for the aggressors. Then one of the attackers, "in a final sadistic gesture . . . shoved his fingers deep into the boy's rectum and ripped out a mass of bloody hemorrhoids." [31] Laite was shocked by the unconcern shown by the guards. He stated that the "guards were protected from the violent prisoners, but I, an inmate myself, was not. The guards never made an attempt to discipline the prisoners. In fact I suspected that they might pass the time of day watching the fights and sexual activities from some secluded location." [32] This sexual attack is not the exception in jail, for Davis cited over two thousand assaults in his study, and one need only read his accounts to know that they were not much more *palatable* than the one described by Laite.

Mode of Dress

In free society most men prefer to dress modestly in the presence of other men and more especially when women are in the vicinity. This is not true when men find themselves confined to penal institutions.

The training schools and detention centers are probably the only correctional institutions that do not issue uniforms to their residents. Each boy wears what he receives from home, and this often leads directly to sexual exploitation it-

---

[30] *Ibid.,* p. 43.
[31] *Ibid.,* p. 44.
[32] *Ibid.,* p. 128.

self. It is a common event for some inmate to desire an item
of clothing belonging to another inmate. If the item desired
cannot be stolen from the unsuspecting owner, then the aggressor seeks to make it his through some threat of physical
abuse or sexual exploitation.

The phenomenon of semi-naked appearance is not considered abnormal in a training school, especially in the summer
when bermuda shorts and tank tops, or no tops at all, are
worn both by the staff and the inmates. This mode of dress
does not appear to *turn one inmate on* to another in a physical sense of the term. The same cannot be said of conditions
existing in maximum security institutions.

In most reformatories, jails, and prisons, uniforms are
issued to the inmates and are to be worn under pain of disciplinary measures if the rule is violated. However, due to
the age of most penal institutions, they are hot boxes in the
summer, and in the winter they become virtual steam rooms
because windows and fans are sealed up and antiquated boil-
ers run at their only temperature setting—high. Therefore,
men will seek to strip off as much clothing as possible in
order to be comfortable. Others, such as weight lifters, have a
propensity to show off what muscles they have by walking
around nude to the waist most of the time; while those with
exotic and erotic tattoos remain in a semi-naked state so that
other inmates will be able to attest to their 'virility' by making comments about the multi-colored sagas stained on their
skin.

Laite was dumbfounded by the dress habits of the men
with whom he was confined. He stated, "Their nakedness
and seminakedness was something I had not expected, and I
found it blatantly, almost savagely offensive. . . . It was several days before I began to get used to seeing them in the
nude. . . . Some stayed completely naked most of the time.
The others were usually bare from the waist up." [33]

It appears that the correctional staff in most institutions
does little to enforce the rule of proper dress, possibly due to

[33] *Ibid.*, p. 122.

the fact that it is virtually impossible to go around all day telling men to put their clothes on, but more probably because the guards in too many institutions simply do not care to enforce the dress code. Thus, physical awareness of inmates, especially among the jocks and wolves interested in young lean bodies, is heightened to the point of making sexual assault almost a normal and expected event in this type of setting.

Reformatory Setting

The reformatory is the graduate school of institutions for young offenders (16-28 years old). Having passed through detention centers, training schools, and even jails, they have made it to the big time when sentenced to the reform school. This is no unimportant fact and weighs heavily on the status that a young offender will have when he later leaves the institution to return home. He is considered somewhat of a tough guy by his chums at home, especially those who may have served sentences with him in the training school or detention center, because now they look up to him as the tough who got sent up to the big house—the reformatory.

The fact that he has been sentenced to a maximum security institution with other young offenders is also important to the inmate himself, for now he is expected to establish a reputation among his fellow inmates that will also receive acclaim from the boys back home when he returns on parole or is released after serving his time. One of the ways of establishing a name is through sexual exploitation, a goal to which the physical setting of most reformatories lends itself in a most accommodating manner.

The Connecticut Reformatory is divided into three wings housing inmates on a merit system that rewards the offender for good behavior by placing him in sections of the institution where living accommodations are more private and habitable. The main section of the reformatory consists of four hundred cells piled one on top of another like so many bird cages. Four stories high, this wing constitutes the first stage of living quarters for newly admitted inmates. It is here that the inmate must fight to keep his manhood.

The cell block is several hundred feet long and the cages are built within the building itself, separated from the surrounding outer walls in such a manner as to give the appearance of a cage within a cage, for the outer windows on the walls are also barred for extra security. It is within this setting that many sexual attacks occur, due to the size of the installation, the lack of adequate coverage by custodial staff, as well as neglect of duties on the part of some of the officer staff itself.

It is almost impossible for one inmate to sexually exploit another without the assistance of another inmate or group of inmates. There is a rare exception wherein the aggressor is so physically powerful that he can overpower the victim without assistance of any kind. However, solo attack is a distinct disadvantage to the aggressor since he will not have witnesses to the act of domination imposed on his victim, and this is as important as the act itself. In this cell block setting, oral sexual acts are usually the price paid by the victim, since anal sodomy would require stripping of clothing and positions not conducive to the physical structure of the block itself. In most instances the group of inmates will be served by the victim after he has satisfied the jock. In this way the group will keep watch while the others take their turns in the sexual act. Even if the victim should rebel during the attack, there is little chance that the attackers will be found in the act, for the distance that the officers must travel to the farthest section of the cell block is a considerable one; if the attack occurs on the third story of the cage, it is almost impossible for an officer to witness the aggressive behavior taking place. Without this witnessing by the officer, there can be no formal accusation made against the aggressor should the victim decide to press charges. This is rarely the case since the victim would only suffer more aggressive attacks should he decide to make a complaint to the authorities.

In the evening security crews are numerically half that of the day staff since the inmates are locked in for the night and the daily routines of classes, shops, and other programs are not in progress. Security is at its most lax point and it is a prime occasion for exploitation to occur. During the hours right after supper and just before the final evening break when inmates are allowed to walk in the yard, the cell block is a major target for sexual exploitation. The changing of the guard is taking place and many inmates are coming and going to their cells. I have found that rapists are more often found in the cell block area than in any other part of the institution. This fact has been somewhat corroborated by Roth in his studies as well.[34]

The section of the reformatory used for classes was another area where exploitation could and did occur rather frequently. Here again, the third floor was vacant and the inmates were at ease since there were only two teachers conducting classes and policing the area. The weaker inmates were made to perform sexual acts against their will; only in this setting, anal sodomy was the price paid because the isolation of the class area itself accommodated this type of exploitive activity.

The shop area of the reformatory was most assuredly notorious for sexual acts including oral sex, *leggins,* and anal intercourse. Extremely large in area and relatively unprotected, it was a perfect setting for sexual exploitation. Not only was the area isolated, but an extremely unwilling inmate could be rendered totally helpless since there were always ropes, chains, and other items that could be used to restrain or silence a struggling victim, and they were used more frequently than not by the aggressors.

The shower room was a place where weaker inmates were made to submit to both oral and anal sex at once, with others waiting in line for their own gratification. The aggressors had a unique method of camouflage, and here again they were assisted by the age of the building itself. There were no

---

[34] Dr. Lauren H. Roth, "Territoriality and Homosexuality in a Male Prison," *American Journal of Orthopsychiatry,* 41:511-512 (1971). Roth found that most rapists are concentrated in the cell block area of a prison and that they "roam unchallenged by other predators surrounded by the prey of his species."

éxhaust fans in the shower room and by turning the showers at the farthest end of the room to their maximum hot capacity, a true and impenetrable cloud of steam formed in the back of the room. When the custodial officer occasionally glanced into the room, he saw normal bathing activities occurring in the foremost section of the stall, while in the rear, behind this ingenious screen, some weaker inmate was being made to satisfy several aggressors, amid the more obvious talk and bawdy comments being made by those faking their routine within visual contact of the security guard.

Medical Experimentation Adds to Sexual Exploitation

In many of our prisons [35] in the United States, pharmaceutical houses, medical schools, and private foundations, test drugs and other products on the inmate population, with their written consent. The very nature of this type of experimentation adds to the chances of sexual exploitation as vividly demonstrated by Davis in his study in Philadelphia. He found that the University of Pennsylvania and a private concern operated a large laboratory for testing new drugs as well as experimental products such as shaving creams and toilet tissue on prisoners. The inmates received compensation for this experimentation and an experienced assistant earned as much as "100 dollars a month, in prison economy, the equivalent of a millionaire's income." [36] With this earning power goes the ability to buy what the holder of this money desires, and many times that is the body of another inmate. This is especially true since only those inmates who work are paid. If a man is without a job and without outside money from his family, he is at the mercy of those who have the goods he wants. Davis is explicit in his indictment of this medical experimentation when he says that "the project contributed to homosexuality in the prison." [37]

The individual who ran the project, with the power to de-

---

[35] Jessica Mitford, "Experiments Behind Bars," *Atlantic Magazine*, 321:64-73 (January, 1973). A thorough account of experimentation in prison.

[36] Davis, *op. cit.*, p. 14.

[37] *Ibid.*

cide which inmates would serve as subjects for the tests, was himself an inmate. Davis states that "Randall's taste was newly admitted young inmates. Through his influence with the guard staff, he had his pick of these young men assigned to him as cell mates, and for as long as he wished. When his victims moved in, Randall solicited them to engage in sexual acts in return for 'getting them on the tests.' At least half a dozen inmates submitted." [38] When Davis questioned the guards as to why Randall had his choice of inmates, he was told that the *higher ups* had instructed the guards not to interfere with the inmates working for the University of Pennsylvania project. In a final and almost unbelievable statement Davis states that "it is the duty of prison officials to reduce the economic power that any inmate might exercise over another inmate. Yet . . . prison officials, either through neglect or indifference, disregarded this duty. As a result, at least one inmate became so economically powerful that he was able to choose as cell mates, a series of young men he found attractive, and then use bribery to sexually subvert each one." [39]

Researchers in Connecticut's correctional system have found that the reason for inmates taking part in these tests is "universally declared that money was the prime motive for volunteering—even at unfair rates." [40] In light of what Davis found, it is not mere hypothetical exaggeration to wonder how many similar situations of sexual exploitation occur where these types of experiments and the financial system they support are in existence; the fact is that over forty-five [41] of our correctional centers in the nation allow this type of experimentation.

---

[38] *Ibid.*

[39] *Ibid.*, p. 13.

[40] Lawrence Alberts and Thomas A. DeRiemer, "Connecticut Watchdogs Human Research Experiments," *American Journal of Correction*, 35:43 (March-April, 1973).

[41] Jessica Mitford, "Experiments Behind Bars," *Atlantic Magazine*, 321:69 (January, 1973).

Staff Involvement in Sexual Exploitation

Davis raises the issue of officer implication in the exploitation suffered by inmates in correctional institutions. The shocking fact is that there is both overt and covert implication of officers in the attacks that take place in penal institutions. At the least the "inmates have little faith in the ability of guards to protect them from retaliation should they complain (about sexual assaults). Their fears are justified by the lack of supervision by guards and the inadequate facilities to provide security for complainants." [42] These facts are apparently common knowledge since "cases and studies dealing with homosexual abuses in prison show that these sexual practices are well known and common throughout the United States prisons. Victims are at the mercy of their aggressors and receive little protection from prison authorities who are in charge of their safe keeping." [43] Equally as tragic for the weaker inmates is the implicit agreement reached by personnel of each institution concerning what actions they will allow in the way of sexual attack within the walls of their institution. For in truth "the bargain that is finally struck in any penal institution between the inmates, the custodial staff and the professional-rehabilitative staff will be the major institutional factor effecting the sexual adjustments of the inmate population, for this bargain represents the degree of control of individual behavior (both staff and inmate) that the institution demands." [44]

Sagarin and MacNamara have stated that a "number of descriptions of . . . prison rapes have occurred in the literature, both scientific and popular. The victim is almost always young, and the event itself hardly seems possible without the connivance, or at least purposeful inattention, of prison authorities." [45] Further, these authors also state that "some

[42] Davis, *op. cit.*, p. 11.

[43] "Sexual Assaults and Forced Homosexual Relationships in Prison: Cruel and Unusual Punishment," *Albany Law Journal*, 36:438, 1972.

[44] Buffum, *op. cit.*, p. 6.

[45] Edward Sargarin and Donal E. J. MacNamara, *The Homosexual As a Crime Victim*. A paper presented at the First International Symposium on Victimology, Hebrew University, Jerusalem, Israel, September 2-6, 1973, p. 37.

homosexual inmates and ex-inmates (claim) that they have been utilized as gifts by prison officials to prisoners who toe the line, keep order, and make it possible for a prison administration to run smoothly." [46] Further, they relate an incident by an ex-inmate who was in his late twenties when incarcerated. He claims to have been "presented to an entire wing of the prison as a bonus to the convicts for their good behavior during the previous months. In this wing, any prisoner who wanted his services, at any time for any purpose, was given it, the guards opening doors, passing him from one cell to another, providing lubricants, permitting two convicts to have simultaneous sexuality (oral and anal) when this was desired, and even arranging, for those requiring it, some privacy." [47] The same authors also cite claims that guards themselves engage in "sodomistic assaults on prisoners, or (induce) reluctant prisoners to permit sexual activities upon them in return for favors, protection, and other rewards." [48]

Comments by Davis reveal that many guards discourage complaints by victims of sexual assaults, by indicating that they did not want to be bothered. One victim screamed for over an hour while he was being gang raped in his cell; the block guard ignored the screams and laughed at the victim when the rape was over. The inmates who reported this passed a polygraph examination. The guard who had been named refused to take the test.[49] It appears that the guards often pressured victims not to complain for it would indicate that they were not doing their duty. Often they used the tactic of asking the victim of an attack if he wanted his parents and friends to find out about his humiliation.[50] The same indictment of officer exploitation of certain inmates for

---

[46] *Ibid.,* p. 39.

[47] *Ibid.,* pp. 39-40. These authors are careful to state that this testimony was without corroboration and may have been embellished by the bitterness of the former inmate. Yet, they cite the incident as highly plausible.

[48] *Ibid.,* p. 40. Again, the authors comment about a paucity of corroboration in this incident.

[49] Davis, *op. cit.,* p. 11.

[50] *Ibid.*

Rape in Prison

sexual reasons is reported by Dintz, Miller, and Bartollas, who state that "unfortunately some guards will barter their weaker and younger charges to favored inmates in return for inmate cooperation in keeping the prison under control." [51]

Nor is this involvement in sexual exploitation limited only to the line guards and officers, for it has been substantiated that in one Southern Institution an inmate could buy a "kid" from a guard for the right price. These young boys were won and lost in crap games for less than fifty dollars. At this institution, if one had the money, he could buy a kid from Robert Hock, the Deputy Warden, if the buyer met the price and was liked by Hock,[52] himself.

It is obvious that "this kind of violence has usually been covertly encouraged by the institutional staff. It is not the work of disturbed youths, or mess-ups, instead, it must be seen as a basic feature of the social organization of correctional institutions." [53]

---

[51] Simon Dinitz, Stuart J. Miller, and Clemens Bartollas, *Inmate Exploitation—A Study on the Juvenile Victim*. A paper presented to the First International Symposium on Victimology, Hebrew University, Jerusalem, Israel, September 2-6, 1973, p. 2.

[52] Jack Griswold, Mike Misenheimer, and Art Powers, *An Eye For An Eye*, Tromanhauser, ed. (New York, Holt, Rinehart and Winston, 1970), pp. 42, 43.

[53] Don C. Gibbons, "Violence in American Society: The Challenge To Corrections," *The American Journal of Correction*, 31:8 (March-April, 1969).

CHAPTER **3**

MALE AGGRESSION AND SEXUAL ACTS

As matters now stand, sex is unquestionably the most pertinent issue to the inmates' life behind bars.

Jack L. Ward

FOR JUST A MOMENT as I read a horrendous account of rape in the local newspaper, I am outraged, and like others in our community, find it difficult to comprehend any rationale for such an act. Yet, this behavior is even more common in the prisons, jails, and reformatories (all now called correctional centers) in which I have practiced my vocation as teacher and counselor. These sexual acts include closeted adolescent experiments, voluntary one-to-one homosexual relationships, as well as the violent and politically significant act of rape. I am certainly not alone in my concern about the relationship between violence and sex that occurs among our youth. There are those who believe that "violence, all violence, is both sexual and political in character, and that its explanation lies in the psychosexual disfigurement of the young male. For violence . . . in the United States is indisputedly synonymous with young male aggression; murder, rape and assault, (and) gratuitous brutality." [1]

Implicit in these observations is the view that a variety of sexual preferences exists among all juveniles. These include heterosexual, homosexual, bisexual and asexual choices. Throughout these observations it is to be understood that

---

[1] Doston Rader, "The Sexual Nature of Violence," *New York Times,* October 22, 1973, p. C-31.

33

sexual behavior, relative to hypersexuality, remains in a hypothetical state at best. This is true even in the average community in which we live, for there appears to be no one single answer to the sexual drive in its heightened state. Many of these young men (in correctional institutions) see themselves as hypersexual and credit this to the fact that they are institutionalized. Yet, they freely attest to the fact that they practiced the same behavior before institutionalization, and many return to the same modes of sexual expression when released. Others choose to adopt the new sexuality they learned while confined. In most instances the younger generation (14 to 25 years of age) view sexual behavior as a mixture of feelings and actions, and there is little or no shame about expressing these feelings in pairs or in groups, with males or females. "What has been happening recently is that our young people have been assuming more responsibility for their own sexual standards and behavior. In short, today's more permissive sexual standards represent not revolution . . . (but) normality. There has been a gradually increasing acceptance of and overtness about sexuality. In the next decade, we can expect a step-up in the pace of this change." [2]

Relationships

"Most delinquents have the same habits and needs and respond to the same array of human experiences which influence the majority of us." [3] Therefore, it is reasonable to believe that residents of training schools, reformatories, and other correctional institutions have the same basic sexual needs as normal non-institutionalized adolescents.[4] However, one may question the manner in which the inmate expresses his needs if in fact confinement really affects this expression

[2] Ira I. Reiss, *Studies In Human Sexual Behavior: The American Scene,* Ailon Shiloh, ed. (Springfield, Charles C Thomas, 1970), p. 28.

[3] Richard J. Clenden, "Whats Wrong With Corrections," *Federal Probation,* 35:9 (1971).

[4] James F. Short and Ivan F. Nye, "Extent of Unrecorded Juvenile Delinquency, Tentative Conclusions," in James E. Teele, *Juvenile Delinquency A Reader* (Itasca, F. E. Peacock, 1970), pp. 10-16.

as much as is believed by the public. It is my belief that institutionalization, in large measure, only reflects what occurs all too often in the free outside community. Confinement does not cause the differing modes of expression; they were inherent and in many instances practiced by the inmate before he was sentenced.

Relationships in most correctional centers inevitably are based on a one-to-one male relationship, sexuality being only one aspect of this association. Whether a young man seeks social, psychological, or sexual fulfillment or experimentation, it is with another male that this function is performed. Therefore, a homosexual life style becomes part of the institutional way of life, be it overt or covert, voluntary or forced. I have stressed the need for women in correctional centers as teachers, counselors, and paraprofessionals so as to make the setting more normal for the all-male population.[5] Where feasible, coed forms of corrections should be instituted to make the setting totally integrated—male and female.

For the administrator, homosexual phenomena (and heterosexual aggression) represents potential for violent clashes among men seeking sexual and personalized outlets in other than the socially acceptable manner. At a more intense level, homosexual behavior has carried a potential for murder and riots within institutions.[6] In spite of these obvious facts, "there is a lack of investigation into the nature and meaning of homosexual behavior in juvenile institutions."[7] This obvious lack of study on such a crucial question is even more incredible when one considers that "as matters now stand, sex is unquestionably the most pertinent issue in the inmates' life behind bars."[8] This is no new revelation. As early as 1948 Kinsey realized the importance of the effect that institu-

---

[5] Dr. Anthony M. Scacco, Jr., "Some Observations About Women and Their Role in the Field Of Corrections," *The American Journal Of Correction,* 34:10-12 (March-April, 1972).

[6] Jack L. Ward, "Homosexual Behavior of the Institutionalized Delinquent," *Psychiatric Quarterly Supplement,* 32:301 (1958).

[7] *Ibid.*

[8] *Ibid.,* p. 302.

tions have on young men when he said, "if these adolescent years are spent in an institution where there is little or no opportunity for the boy to develop his individuality, where there is essentially no privacy at any time of the day, and where all his companions are other males, his sexual life is very likely to become stamped with the institutional pattern." [9] It is precisely this pattern that the administrators and the public are, in large part, unwilling to discuss and the reason why the area of sexuality within correctional institutions remains in a state of limbo.

Masturbation

Probably the most common release for sexual tension within a correctional institution is masturbation. Here again, there is no cause for alarm; most of the male population has its first experience in self-relief after the age of ten, with an estimated 13 to 16 percent having masturbated before this age. There is a further note of *normalcy* when one considers that 99 percent of young men and women masturbate occasionally, while the hundredth conceals the truth. Moll stated that "the only point in dispute is whether there are any exceptions." [10] Within the institutions themselves, adolescents attest to this mode of relief in a competitive and almost public frame of mind. The eleven to fourteen-year-olds stated that they masturbate four and even more times during the week.[11] Here again, an act that is considered by adults to be private is performed in a most open manner.[12]

The boys let one another know that they are going to seek

---

[9] Alfred C. Kinsey, Wardell B. Pomeroy, and Clyde E. Martin, *Sexual Behavior in the Human Male* (Philadelphia, W. B. Sanders, 1948), p. 224.

[10] Albert Moll (1912) a physicial-sexologist . . . was willing to give the benefit of the doubt to some males. Havelock Ellis "His Studies in the Psychology of Sex," determined the 99%. *The Encyclopedia of Sexual Behavior*, Albert Ellis and Albert Abarbanel eds. (New York, Hawthorne Books, 1967), pp. 54-55.

[11] Personal conversations by the author with the boys involved in these observations at the training school.

[12] *A Handbook Of Correctional Psychiatry*, Vol. 1 (Washington, D.C., Superintendent of Documents, U.S. Government Printing Office, U.S. Bureau Prisons, Department Justice, 1968), p. 11.

relief by masturbating. A verbal announcement is made to this effect and the boys attempt to see who can ejaculate first. This type of activity is done by each boy, some in visual proximity of others, but with plenty of audible conversation relative to the various stages of excitement, until ejaculation is accomplished. The challenge is in reaching climax before the others, and waiting to see who can achieve orgasm next. This form of behavior is continued until those who are participating have given verbal testimony that they have discharged successfully. There are more than a few remarks relative to the amount of sperm ejaculated. Thus, the boys appear to place emphasis on the amount of time it takes to climax and on the amount of sperm that results from this sexual activity. Some of the boys refer to their girl friends during these actions, while others make remarks about their desire for another inmate. The point of all this is simply that these activities are happening to young men who are at the height of their sexual prowess, and it happens in a vacuum. The staff either ignores what they know to be occurring, or worse, refuses to admit that "this type of thing occurs in our institution."

I am not suggesting punishing those who seek sexual relief in this manner; I believe that the boys of this age, in most instances, would like to discuss their feelings with those sympathetic to their needs, even their sexual needs.

Two very common events in training school are known as the *hand shake* and *leggins*. The former is a form of mutual masturbation, usually taking place quickly, as it can be done whenever privacy and security are present in disproportionate amounts. Each boy relieves the other, using their hands in this action. The latter is a method where the boys insert one another's penis between their legs, usually while in a standing position. This form of sex play is more difficult because of the position involved and the need to outwit security procedures and personnel, one of the reasons why it is so challenging to the boys who seek this mode of sexual play. Areas such as clothing rooms, attics, deserted stairwells, and unsupervised showers provide the necessary cover for these quick acts of sexual gratification.

Masturbation in a Reformatory Setting

Masturbation in a reformatory takes on a totally new dimension. This is due to the fact that sentences are longer, the age group is older (16 to 21 years old), security is more stringent, and many of the inmates have been sentenced to the same institution two or three times so they know they have to serve their sentence before they can seek sexual relief on the outside. The very nature of their incarceration affects their mode of sexual expression.

Reformatories are considered to be maximum security institutions because they are usually walled or fenced, and have sentinel towers with armed guards and/or sophisticated electronic sensing devices to discourage escapes. The training school has none of these elaborate precautions and is considered to be an open institution. Also, visiting regulations in a reformatory are not as liberal as those in a training school. The reformatory allows no hours, days or weekends off for home visits. Only recently have visitors even been allowed to be in close physical proximity to their relatives. Therefore, the inmate, as a result of all these security precautions, has a more intense need for for sexual gratification in this type of institution.

Much of the self-satisfaction sought is accomplished in one's own "house," the nickname given by the inmates to their cells. It is against the rules to talk after lights out, but conversation goes on loud and clear from cell to cell and tier to tier after the final bulb is out. Men will begin to challenge each other to see who reaches climax first, while cat calls from the more effeminate inmates can be heard in the background during these sessions. I wish to emphasize the word *effeminate,* for the inmates have what I consider a peculiar sense of what constitutes manhood and womanhood. It is their assumption that a biological male is to be considered womanly if he lisps, walks with a slight swagger, or manifests other forms of behavior considered womanly. Yet, upon questioning, these same individuals will state that these *queens*, the name given to those they consider to be effeminate, are, after all, like the queens they see on the outside. Again, an example of institutional jargon being imported from the outside.

The act of masturbation is punishable, usually by sentencing the inmate to the hole, a name given to a separate solitary lock-up cell. Prior to 1968 in Connecticut, confinement in the hole meant that the individual was stripped, given no mattress, and if he was an extremely difficult discipline problem, no toilet paper. Also, his day's portion of food was severely limited, almost to a handful thrown on a plate. Although the hole still exists, these severe physical limitations have been largely suspended but the psychological punishment remains.

Detection of self-induced sexual play is made more possible through the actual construction of one particular cell block. The housing for approximately three hundred inmates consists of four tiers of cells piled on top of each other. Each level has inner corridors that run the length of each tier. From these inner halls each cell can be observed individually through small peep holes. The standard joke among the guards used to be catching the inmates masturbating and then taking the necessary steps toward punishment.

Mutual masturbation in this setting is usually confined to the shower rooms and shop areas where security is reduced and where other inmates can act as a cover. The shower rooms are usually supervised but we have already seen that the inmates are inventive enough to relieve each other quite successfully without being detected. Also, soap has more than a cleaning purpose, and serves equally as well as a lubricant for sexual play among any two or more men. The shop areas are more prone to support involved sexual play such as leggins and sodomy. As with any institution, there are those officers who do their assigned jobs and those who are not as conscientious. As security suffers in these areas, so do many of the inmates, for not all the sex that occurs is voluntary.

Oral Sexual Gratification—Training School

It appears that younger boys, eleven to sixteen years old,
approach the subject of oral sex with levity, hidden by the
desire to prove their sexual prowess.[13] This type of activity is
more risky because of the lowering of clothing and necessary
position. In spite of this, it is practiced many times. Of the
sixteen youths taking part in fellatio, three said they reached
climax. It is of significance that most of the boys registered
verbal disgust, even physical threats, toward the boy who had
provided the service for their satisfaction. However, they had
all entered into the act frequently during the course of one
month during which these observations were made; one can
question whether their verbal expressions of disgust were
truly sincere or indeed were only part of the macho* reputations they feel compelled to uphold as a result of being in the
presence of the other inmates. They consistently want to appear as if they are heterosexually oriented, when in fact their
behavior within the institution and that prior to confinement
certainly leads one to believe that at the least they have
heard and/or seen homosexual behavior, and in many instances have taken part in male sex and enjoyed what they
were doing.[14] Kinsey appropriately expressed the more sensible interpretation of the actions of these boys when he
said, "Males do not represent two discrete populations heterosexual and homosexual. The world is not to be divided
into sheep and goats. Not all things are black and white (for)
nature rarely deals with discrete categories. Only the human

---

* Macho (Machismo) is a slang term from the Spanish used to connote manhood or virility. In the 50's it was the D.A. haircut and leather jackets. Today
it might be the hippie look, the long hair as well as other trappings. See John
Irwin, *The Felon* (Englewood, Prentice Hall, 1970), p. 81.

[13] Kinsey, *et al., op. cit.* Kinsey stresses the importance of physical signs and
development as marking the breaking point between patterns of sexual activity of the pre-adolescent boys and patterns of the older adult boy.

[14] Albert Reiss, "Social Integration of Queers and Peers," in Donald
Cressey, *Delinquency, Crime and the Social Processes* (New York, Harper and
Row, 1960), p. 996. Reiss tells how the boys from the lower socioeconomic
class in large cities are prepared to make contact with fellators and relate to
them. They learn this from other boys in the delinquent subculture.

mind invents categories and tries to force facts into separate pigeon holes. The living world is a continuum in each and every one of its aspects. The sooner we learn this concerning human sexual behavior, the sooner we shall reach a sound understanding of the realities of sex." [15] Kinsey's statement is more important when we consider that 818 males, age eleven years and older that he studied, fell into the category determined to be "equally heterosexual and homosexual," [16] and this as early as 1948. It is obvious that with increased sexual freedom and expression, these statistics would be greatly enlarged in the 1970's. Yet, nothing is done within institutions to study sexuality in spite of the apparent need.

The boys in the cottage* at the training school obtained sexual gratification in a group in the recreation room of their building. The individual providing the service knelt and *did* every one of the boys, except four. It is note worthy that full sexual play occurred during the day when staff coverage was supposed to be at its peak. Further, when these actions were brought to the attention of the staff, a meeting was held and the boys admitted to their conduct with little or no guilt; this fact completely shocked the staff which included a nun. Again, this is an example of the boys seeing nothing wrong in doing on the inside what they freely do on the outside. The boys blamed the inmate who satisfied them for providing the opportunity for them to act out their sexual desires. It is ironic that the staff took a similar view, stating this probably never would have occurred if the fellator was not in their cottage. The entire matter of the acts having taken place at all and among such a large number of boys was completely overlooked. Finally, the staff found it necessary to chide the boys as a group and to restrict the movements, not of the cottage as a whole, but only of the fellator, so that the incident would not happen again.

---

* Cottage, This is the name given to the homes in which the boys live. There is usually a male and female (sometimes husband and wife) to act as cottage parents. The inmates live as well as attend school in the cottage. In short, it is a self-contained housing and educational unit.

[15] Kinsey, *et al., op. cit.,* p. 639.

[16] *Ibid.*

It is obvious that the boy performing the act was singled out for punishment, again a carry-over on the part of the staff because outside society also has a tendency to punish the one performing or soliciting the act.[17] In addition, the staff agreed that the fellator was to have his hair cut in order to make him more masculine, as they thought his shoulder length hair to be a temptation to the others. Also, he was to wear more masculine clothing. He had been wearing dyed dungarees with designs he had put on them, as well as seeing to it that they fit snugly, something the other boys also did, but they were given no orders to alter their behavior or their clothing. Finally, he was never to be allowed alone with any of the other boys, nor be left unsupervised in the cottage. All these precautions were upheld by the members of the staff for three or four days. Then, as time wore thin, so did the dedication of the staff, and the fellator and the other boys returned to their sexual games.

Before leaving this particular case I would like to make it known that many of the boys admitted to having oral sex performed on them while on the outside and for money. Some took pride in the fact that they knew where homosexuals could be found and made the most of this information. "After all" said one of the boys, "it is an easy way to make money without having to rip anybody off [rob them] and it's one way for a guy to satisfy himself. Besides, all the guys do it. It's O.K. as long as you never go down on anybody yourself." [18] (that is perform the act, rather than having it performed on oneself)

Oral Sex Within a Reformatory

Here again sex is more torrid relative to oral gratification. In the reformatory being described here, the young men stated that more often than not there are queens avail-

---

[17] Albert J. Reiss, Jr., "The Social Integration of Queers and Peers," in Donald R. Cressey and David A. Ward, *Delinquency, Crime and the Social Processes* (New York, Harper and Row, 1960), p. 1008.

[18] Personal conversation with one of the boys involved in the observations at the training school.

able for such acts. I have spoken little of forced oral sexual acts, but these are quite prevalent in a reformatory setting. Sex is often used to force a debtor to repay an obligation he cannot pay for in kind. So he is subjected to humiliation in the form of this act in front of other inmates. The inmate in question may have borrowed too many cigarettes, a debt payable on a two to one basis; perhaps he has lost his commisary privileges and has asked another inmate to loan him certain commodities which he cannot now repay. Or perhaps the inmate is simply considered as sexually desirable by some stud * with a reputation for getting what he wants, or as we have seen in the recent riot at Attica, the act may be political in nature. Two white men (among many) had to pay the political price at the hands of some black men when one inmate testified that "what has not come out yet, but will soon, is that the rebels brutally and repeatedly raped two young white kids (themselves not homosexuals), at knife point. They held knives at their throats and forced them to submit to oral and anal sodomy at the same time. They also did that to several other white kids, but I know the two I write about." [19] I have stated earlier that reformatories are like prisons and the analogy is valid in this instance also.

Let no one be deceived, therefore, for reformatories are maximum security lockups; let no one be further deceived, for it is merely a matter of checking the statistical record to learn that racial strife is often brought on by sexual pressures, pressures that an informed staff could avoid had they taken the time, and even more tragically, if they would not merely turn their heads the other way relative to conditions now existing in correctional centers. It is important here again to quote Kinsey, who administrators have yet to heed, for he said:

the problem of sexual adjustment for a younger male who is confined to mental, penal, or other sort of institution is even

---

* Stud is the name usually given to the individual taking the male role in a sexual act.

[19] Fredrick Wiggins, "The Truth About Attica by an Inmate," *National Review*, 24:329 (March 31, 1972).

more difficult than the problem of the boy who lives outside in society. Administrators who have these younger males in their care are generally bewildered and at a loss to know how to handle their sexual problems. In many cases the situation is simply tolerated or ignored and the administrator would prefer not to be aware of the activities. For this, many people would condemn him; but the problem in an institution for teen-age boys is far more complex than the public or the administration . . . have realized.[20]

Sodomy in a Training School

Anal intercourse among eleven to fourteen-year-olds in a male correctional institution is more prevalent than believed. The particular group of boys described here was unique in having an avowed homosexual as well as a clinically diagnosed transexual in its population. Gifts, sometimes cigarettes and more often money, were given to the boys that were being bought for their sexual prowess. Those who allowed sodomy to be performed on themselves evidently enjoyed the act and one of the boys stated that he thought the other guys were nice looking. He also commented that he frequently was *had* on the outside and was used to it. One of the residents seemed to have summed up the general feeling toward this form of sexuality. He was of the opinion that "some of the boys like it both ways here and on the outside. I don't know why the old people (staff) think that a guy can't want another guy, even if he makes it with his girl friend also. Besides, its none of their goddamn business what a guy wants and what he does, in here or on the outside." [21] It is obvious that this inmate did not think these forms of sexuality were being performed by sick or deranged fellow inmates. Kinsey seems to support this view since he stated that "37 percent of American males had had at least one homosexual experience and that 4 percent of them are exclusively homosexual." [22] This would seem to

---

[20] Kinsey, *et al., op. cit.,* p. 224.

[21] Personal conversation with one of the inmates involved in the observations made at the training school.

[22] Kinsey, *et al., op. cit.,* p. 224.

confirm that the pattern is not the sole prerogative of deviants, criminals, or those institutionalized.

In the cottage that housed boys fifteen to seventeen years old, the same cannot be said about no forced acts of sex. These boys were from poor economic backgrounds, as well as fragmented homes, complicated by ghetto conditions. Also, the cottage held more blacks than Puerto Ricans or whites. More than one story of rape emanated from this cottage. The sole one mentioned here is an act of sodomy forced upon a Puerto Rican youth by two black residents. This reference is by no means meant to imply that only blacks rape Puerto Ricans, for sex knows no color barrier. As psychologist Ralph Garofalo has stressed, "the rapist [speaking of male-female rape] is not an exotic freak; in some cases his behavior is merely an extreme manifestation of the normal sex drive . . . the crucial distinction . . . is that normal men find a socially acceptable outlet for their desires, while the rapist loses all sight of moral or legal considerations." [23] Evidently, the older boys at this training school lost sight of moral considerations rather frequently as do their counterparts in jails and prisons. The rape was performed with others in the cottage aware of the situation, but who did nothing to stop it either because they were afraid of being raped themselves or were merely disinterested in what common procedure was when one boy was taken by another. The two boys tied a rag gag around the mouth of the victim who struggled against them. He was forced into a clothing room, beaten into submission, stripped, and repeatedly raped.

One of the senior teachers later took time to talk with this author about the sexual acts that occurred in the training school. He stated that as late as 1970, all clothing rooms were off limits as a result of the forced and voluntary sexual acts taking place in them. Also, he said that bathroom call was beyond belief. He said that the element of fear ran high among the boys being intimidated. The stronger boys called

---

[23] "Portrait Of A Rapist," *Newsweek* LXXXII:67-68 (August 20, 1973).

those they forced into sex *bootie boys* since they were forced to kneel and perform oral and anal acts of sex for the aggressors. This type of intimidation caused many of the boys to fight or run the risk of sickening humiliation every time anyone stronger than they desired their body for sexual release. All this is happening, and frequently, in penal institutions today.

In the reformatory setting the forced acts of sex were more brutal in nature, most of the time being performed to let the others know who the dominant and the dominated ones are. Many of the young men were threatened with being stabbed or cut if they did not *give it up*. Although most of the instances of sexual aggression known to this writer were on a one-to-one basis, many forced sexual acts were in the form of gang rapes with the lead stud sharing with the rest of his buddies. Charles Mangel, as late as 1971, could relate such stories as that of "Chuck who saw his first gang rape in a reformatory. A thin blonde kid hung with me, and I watched out for him. One day, sixteen bigger guys caught him alone and raped him in a classroom, beat him silly. I saw a gym teacher rape a kid in an empty swimming pool. Everybody does it. Anyone who's in prison for any length of time and says he doesn't do it by consent or force is a liar." [24] It is of further note that any slightly built young man is sexually approached within hours of his admission to a correctional center, be it a jail, training school, reformatory or prison.[25] The point is startling but true; sex is a major concern of the inmates and yet the administration and staff treat it as being practically nonexistent.

---

[24] Charles Mangel, "How To Make a Criminal Out of a Child," *Look,* 35:51 (June 29, 1971).

[25] *Ibid.*

CHAPTER **4**

THE SCAPEGOAT IS ALMOST ALWAYS WHITE

Racism and Aggression

T HE ISSUE OF RACISM predominates as a central point in
sexual victimization within correctional institutions. It
has even been cited as being "the single most important socio-
demographic characteristic associated with victimization." [1]
These statistics may be due in part to the fact that "in some
states due to higher Negro arrest rates there is a disproportionate number of Negroes relative to the number of Negroes in
the areas from which the prison draws." [2] Again, citing these
statistics, it has been found that there are a disproportionate
number of black aggressors and white victims in studies of
sexual assaults in jails and prisons.[3] What occurs then, is
a definite reversal of the majority and minority roles that
are the natural order in free society. Whether or not there is
black numerical supremacy within the walls of a penal in-

---

[1] Simon Dinitz, Stuart Miller, and Clemens Bartollas, *Inmate Exploitation—
A Study of the Juvenile Victim.* A paper presented to the First International
Symposium on Victimology, Hebrew University, Jerusalem, Israel, September,
1973, p. 9.

[2] Peter C. Buffum, *Homosexuality in Prisons* (Washington, D.C., National
Institute of Law Enforcement and Criminal Justice, U.S. Government Printing
Office, February, 1972), p. 22; Congressman John Conyers, Jr., "The Criminal
Justice System," *The Congressional Record* (House), vol. 119, no. 29, February
22, 1973. "27 percent of all individuals arrested nation wide are black even
though blacks comprise only 11 percent of the total population." p. P.H.-1102.

[3] Alan J. Davis, "Sexual Assaults in the Philadelphia Prison System and
Sheriff's Van," *Transaction* 16:15 (1968).

stitution, the victim is usually not a black but a white or Puerto Rican.

When some of the black aggressors were questioned as to the reasons for making whites submit to sexual acts, their answers were usually that "now it is their turn"; [4] a statement leading one to believe that there are definite socioracial overtones in the act of sexual victimization.

This condition prevailed at the Connecticut School for Boys, a training school for adjudicated juvenile delinquents, which was in fact controlled by the black inmate population, even though they were in the numerical minority. This fact was known to the staff as well as the other inmates. However, as one staff member said, "what can we do? (about the acts of sexual aggression.) If we speak out on behalf of the white boys, the public will say that we are being racists." He went on to explain that officers and correctional personnel were, by their own admission, hesitant to speak out against sex acts being forced on non-blacks for fear of official and community disbelief that blacks could possibly force whites to commit such unnatural acts while they were in confinement and supposedly in the process of being rehabilitated. Further, since the staff was composed of nearly all whites, this staff member was of the opinion that they would simply not be believed by the public in general. Yet, this aggression did occur and is occurring at present in most correctional institutions throughout the nation today.

The population of the training school was housed in cottage dwellings.* Cottage *L* housed the older boys, sixteen to seventeen years old. The only way for a white to survive in this cottage and keep his manhood † intact was to fight. It was not unnatural for a white youth to be unable to defend himself for fear of not being supported by other whites; or as

---

[4] Personal conversation with a black inmate and this author.

* See Chapter 3, *Setting,* for definition of cottage.

† The term *manhood* as used by the inmates, more especially to take one's manhood, is to subject a male to the act of anal sodomy. The aggressor then believes the victim to be taking the role of a woman, in their interpretation, meaning one of subordination.

other researchers have found, completely unwilling "to confront physical threats upon himself with counter violence." [5] He was subject initially to slight humiliation in the form of being called a fag, homo, or perhaps having his brother, sister, or mother spoken of in a derogatory manner. Ultimately (if he was a nonfighter), he was forced to submit to sexual demands by the aggressors, as exploitation and domination were the rule not the exception in this cottage. Authors Miller and Bartollas also found corroborating evidence in their study of 150 young offenders (average age 16.9 years) among whom "pure victims . . . accounted for nearly two out of every five boys," [6] and the majority being victimized were white. Davis adds further insight into the racial aspects of homosexual attack, although in a jail setting, when he found that of the 129 incidents studied: [7]

29 percent involved black offenders and black victims
56 percent involved black offenders and white victims
15 percent involved white offenders and white victims

Among the older boys in the training school, the white victim was always forced to submit to a black in the presence of others so that the white's humiliation and the black's domination could be witnessed. Here again, it has been found that there is a "strong propensity for blacks to fulfill aggressor roles and whites to assume victim roles." [8] Gang rapes were known to have occurred in this cottage, especially among those blacks from urban areas convicted of more serious criminal offenses, such as armed robbery and assault with a deadly weapon.

It should be noted that although the black staff was in the numerical minority relative to the white staff, the former were overtly against any type of aggression by black inmates. In fact, many of the black residents frequently complained that the white boys were privileged relative to themselves.

---

[5] Buffum, *op. cit.*, p. 23.

[6] Dinitz, Miller, and Bartollas, *op. cit.*, p. 4.

[7] Davis, *op. cit.*, p. 15.

[8] Buffum, *op. cit.*, p. 23.

That is, they thought that the whites received special attention and favors when they did not get this attention from
the black staff members. Yet, in spite of this protest, black
counselors and staff would not hesitate to have an overly
aggressive and troublesome black inmate sent to the hole,*
when caught in some act of intimidation against a white or
other black inmate.

Two Puerto Rican inmates in this cottage were relatively
safe from sexual attack. They were from economically and
socially disadvantaged homes and let it be known that they
would fight and use any means to protect themselves from
being sexually intimidated or molested. This factor of social
class and community background appear to influence the
type, as well as the amount of aggression that an individual
will allow to be forced upon himself or force upon others.†

It is interesting to note that Puerto Ricans were in the
numerical minority at the training school; however, should
they desire a sexual outlet, they invariably chose a white
youth to submit to them. Again, bonding between the Puerto
Rican youths was much more closely knit than that of the
whites. It appears that the Puerto Ricans were aware of recent
moves among Spanish speaking inmates to act as a group in
penal institutions. In spite of their age, these Puerto Rican
boys were aware of the fact that the Chicanos, in various
prisons throughout the nation, had formed activist groups,
such as Empleo, which has as its goal a new identity based
on Mexican ancestry and their position of being disadvantaged in white society.[9] These Puerto Rican youths knew that
their Mexican brothers were developing closer ties to the
blacks in correctional centers because they (blacks) were
setting the pace with their militant groups and ideas. It appears that there are other researchers who believe that this
racial-ethic militance and identification will more than likely

---

* *Hole* is defined in Chapter 111, *Male Aggression and Sexual Acts.*

† See Chapter V: *Power and Violence, America's Natural Mode of Expression.*

⁹ John Irwin, *The Felon* (Englewood, Printice Hall, 1970), pp. 80-81.

become increasingly important in the prison world.[10]

Also, the Puerto Ricans, like the blacks, were more willing to run the risk of institutional disciplinary retaliation (however slight it usually was) if they were caught. In contrast, however, the whites rarely bonded together to resist attack or even to form groups that might reverse the sexual aggression being forced upon them and finally, were more conscious of the punishment they would have to endure from the staff if caught even in a fight defending themselves against an aggressor.

Younger Training School Residents

The extent of white victimization in the cottage housing the eleven to fourteen-year-old juveniles was more subtle, yet evident upon investigation. Instead of overtly arranging a time and place where an unassuming white resident of their cottage could be caught unaware, as was frequently the case among the older inmates, these younger boys preferred to play it cool, as one aggressor stated. In the course of a game of cards, or pool, or while taking a shower, one of the black youths might pass a remark about a white inmate concerning the length of his hair, or the size of his penis, or comment about the shape of his buttocks, or the smoothness of his skin. This was always done in a loud manner, using vulgarity to impress the others. One outstanding comment from the blacks in this cottage was that some of the whites did not wear underwear and therefore they (whites) "must be looking for it" (sexual assault). A similar finding was recorded by Davis in his study of the Philadelphia jail where a similar comment preceded a gang rape of a white youth by four blacks.[11]

When a sexual attack did take place among the younger blacks, it was usually oral rather than anal sodomy that was the price paid by their victim. In the cottage housing the older inmates the reverse was more desirable, for the vic-

---

[10] Colt Denfeld and Andrew Hopkins, "Racial-Ethnic Identification in Prisons, Right On from the Inside" (A paper presented at The Eastern Sociological Meeting, Boston, April, 1972), pp. 3-13.

[11] Davis, *op. cit.*, p. 12.

tim to "take it in the rear" was the ultimate form of humiliation and a sign of domination, one that gave the victim a
reputation as long as he remained confined. Also the younger
blacks did not always make it mandatory that the white
youth submit in front of witnesses, as did the older blacks
who seemed primarily concerned with domination and exploitation on the basis that "now whitey knows it is his
turn." Davis also found that conquest and degradation [12] of
the victim were a primary factor in the sexual aggression he
studied. The aggressor used such language as "we're going to
take your manhood," "you'll have to give up some face," and
"we're going to make a girl out of you." [13]

As was stated earlier, the younger blacks did not appear
to engage in sexual aggression primarily for these reasons.
It seemed that as long as the victim was white, this was
enough not only to satiate their appetites, but also to confirm their superiority in the eyes of the other inmates; more
so if the victim was effeminate, according to the general con-
sensus of the other inmates.

The cottage housing these younger inmates had an avowed
white homosexual as well as a clinically diagnosed black
transexual, in its population. The former was fifteen and the
latter fifteen and one-half. The black youth was never forced
into any sexual acts by the other blacks or whites. This may
have been explained by the fact that he was well versed in
street language, rather tall for his age, and considered to
"know the ropes," since he was from one of the larger cities
in Connecticut, and from a ghetto neighborhood. He did,
however, state to this author, that he definitely preferred
white boys who wanted to perform sexual acts on him to
black youths who might have the same intentions. He said
that he was rarely approached by another black for sexual
reasons.

The young white homosexual was not as fortunate as the
black youth just mentioned. He was small and very good
looking, with long blonde hair, frail stature, and known by

---

[12] *Ibid.*, p. 15.
[13] *Ibid.*, p. 16.

the inmate population, as well as the staff, as being a homosexual. Thus, he was victimized by whoever desired his body for physical release or as an act of domination. The white youth in question stated that he liked homosexual activity and preferred well-built white boys, but that he was often forced to provide oral sex for an entire gang of inmates because the act was initiated by one aggressive resident.

When security was at a minimum he engaged in anal sodomy, but most of the sexual relief he granted others was in the form of oral gratification. Once he began any sexual act on a one-to-one basis, he was usually exploited by the others, even those who would normally not partake in this type of activity. This form of group identity, going along with the others in a sexual act, has been verified by Davis who found that "another primary goal of many aggressors, it appears, is to retain membership in the groups led by militant sexual aggressors. This is particularly true of participants in gang rapes. Lacking identification with such groups, as many of the aggressors know, they themselves would become victims." [14]

The Puerto Rican inmates appeared to fare well relative to being the scapegoats for sexual aggressors in general. In fact, when black youths in the cottage were not interested in the white homosexual, the Puerto Ricans were. In two incidents known to this author, sexual play was encouraged by the leader of the cottage, a Puerto Rican youth known for his rather quick temper and physical aggression. He was open in his admiration for the body of the homosexual and let this be known to the staff as well as the other residents of the cottage. He overtly organized a group of the boys to be orally satisfied by the homosexual on two separate occasions. The deserted attic, with its broken security lock, provided a totally secure area for such undetected sexual encounters. This second incident, however, became known to the staff, but as usual, minor disciplinary action was taken against the exploiters, since the staff was of the opinion that the white

[14] *Ibid.*

youth was in reality guilty of enticement. They based this conclusion on the fact that he had to want sex, or they (staff) had no way to explain why so many of the other residents took part in the act. Testimony from the victim showed that he consented because of intimidation, knowing full well the others would resent it if he refused to "take care of them also." He was concerned about the consequences of what would happen should he not consent to the large number who desired to partake in the act. He felt that they would take what they wanted if not given to them freely. This giving in is not at all uncommon, and in larger institutions such as prison, is viewed by the officers as a voluntary commitment on the part of the victim. In reality, however, the inmate desired by the jock or wolf goes along with him in order not to be gang raped at the whim of the marauders wandering within the institution. This happens in all penal institutions, from the minimum security installations, to the maximum security settings. The officers know who the victims are, the administration knows who the victims are, and yet they accept what is happening on a "what can you do basis!" In many instances the guards are directly responsible for fostering sexual aggression within the institutions themselves.*

The reader should not believe that having known homosexuals in correctional centers is unique to Connecticut. In Jennings Hall, one of New York's detention centers for young offenders, similar incidents have developed as a result of the sexual preferences of even the younger inmates for homosexual activity. It was found that "homosexual children are a constant source of potential disruption to the entire program"[15] of rehabilitation.

Many of the whites stated that they would have defended their manhood against the sexual attacks described in these cottage settings, but they accepted the humiliation, in many

---

* See Chapter V: *Power and Violence, America's Natural Mode of Expression,* for further details on this topic.

[15] Peter Kihss, "City Boys' Home Depicted As Base For Criminal Raids," *New York Times,* December 14, 1973, p. L-51.

instances, because they knew that the blacks as well as the Puerto Ricans carried weapons of various sorts. Knives, chains, razors, metal hair picks and in some institutions, homemade guns are not unheard of in the hands of young inmates. Therefore, for a white to resist an attack meant his risking serious injury or mutilation, even if either of these consequences might be the result of an extemporaneous show of force on the part of the aggressor, rather than a planned attack as is usually the situation in large adult penal institutions. Rarely then, were attacks with weapons planned; accidents and injury, in this school, would usually occur when a weapon was glibly flashed as a show of force rather than used as a purposeful instrument to inflict injury. The whites simply did not carry weapons either because they were afraid of institutional rules or simply were not used to weapons as a mode of self-defense. Also the whites did not have the verbal ability, and street savvy, to ward off the baiting techniques of their aggressors. The latter were familiar with institutional settings and knew how to "set up" any white they chose for sexual acts. This was true since most of the aggressors had been returned to the same institution for their second and third time. Thus, they knew how to take what they wanted in the form of sexual gratification. The whites usually had little or no such experience with institutional subcultures and were at a loss as to how to counteract even the slightest act of intimidation directed against them. They were even fooled by such old prison tactics as one black becoming the buddy to a new white inmate to protect him from the others. In reality the aggressor had it planned to make it look as if he were be-friending the newcomer, when in reality he was setting him up in a dependent-like relationship so that when the aggressor had done the white enough favors of protecting him, the latter then owed him, and the way to pay off the debt was to accept anal intercourse.

The reader should be aware that sexual victimization is the final and total act to which a white submits in a penal institution, having been subjected to other more subtle forms of domination initiated by the blacks. Thus, the white scapegoat gives his body up, after he has surrendered his individuality and manhood in many areas; some he may not even be aware of. For example, should a group of whites be watching television and a black enters the room and desires to see another program, he merely changes the station with impunity. Or if the cottage stereo is playing and the black youth prefers some soul music, his choice prevails at the expense of his white and even Puerto Rican fellow inmates. Also, if a white inmate receives some item of clothing or jewelry that is desired by a black youth, it is taken, even in the presence of the victim, with little said or done by the white inmate. In the case of jewelry, the staff attempts to confiscate such items as rings and watches, and keep them in security for the owner until he is released. However, although meant to help the exploited inmates, this rule is sadly enforced and the inmate usually looses it before it can be safely put away for him. In some institutions the black inmates have even affected the choice of food that is served, as in the Tombs in New York, "they have cut down on pork to please the Black Muslims." [16] Should it come, therefore, as a shock to the reader that the black youths will take a white's body for whatever reasons he desires? After all, he has taken whatever else he has desired from the white inmate, why should he not have the youth's body as well?

Another factor in black dominance is the fact that they are usually physically more powerful than the average white at the institution. They tended to be well versed in the art of self-defense and more often than not, spouted slogans that could be identified with black militant groups bent on making the black man aware of his individuality through physical strength and self-assertion. These traits were further heightened by the mutual feeling among black aggressors that "black inmates are proud to be black nowadays. They have a strong sense of race . . . and feel equal to the staff and officers . . . blacks tend to identify with other blacks. If one black is messed with, the entire black population is in-

---

[16] Ted Morgan, "Entombed," *New York Times* Magazine Section 6, February 17, 1974, p. 19.

volved." [17] Here again, any white victim contemplating revenge or at least returning the sexual act to a black aggressor had to bear in mind that a group of blacks might have to be dealt with, not merely the one aggressor who perpetrated the act itself.

White Victimization—Reformatory, Jail, and Prison Setting

Whatever observations or views can be made of victimization in a training school, these incidents are on the lowest rung of the ladder when considered in relationship to that victimization which occurs in jails and reformatories. Prisons have an even more extreme type of aggressive behavior within their walls. Although the youths at the training school were classified by corrections officials and social workers as emotionally unstable, under-educated, socially and culturally disadvantaged, and even dangerous,[18] these young offenders would, at some point, stop short of seriously injuring their victim in a sexual assault. This boundary cannot be said to exist in other penal institutions that carry the label of maximum security settings.

In the reformatory, sentences are longer and the population tends to be older (18 to 21 years). Also, the security is much more stringent, with fifty foot walls and fences enclosing the institution. There are usually turrets mounted on each wall with armed guards, as well as radar and delicate sensory systems designed to detect attempted escapes. Even

---

[17] Denfeld and Hopkins, *op. cit.,* p. 5.

[18] This author knew and worked with Francisco Rodriguez who was classified by the training school as dangerous. The *New York Times* had an article about Francisco under the title *"Boy 16, With Record of Escapes Poses Problem For Connecticut,"* which stated in part that a sixteen-year-old boy who had made frequent escapes from custody, and had escaped again by jumping through an open window in juvenile court where a hearing was being held to send him to a higher security reformatory. His record goes back to his pre-teen years and included assaults with knives and guns, arson, car theft, burglary, purse snatching and drug abuse. Last July 10, he was one of two armed and masked boys who broke his girl friend out of a Bridgeport detention home, at gun point. When picked up by the police, the group was in possession of seventy stolen weapons. *New York Times,* February 23, 1974, p. C-35.

attack dogs, trained to seek out the escapee and hold him until the officers arrive, are standard equipment at many of these institutions. Further, the reformatory offers no opportunity for weekends off, or home visits. (Furloughs are sometimes granted at the end of an inmate's sentence.) Visiting procedures usually take place in a setting wherein the visitor sees the inmate behind a screen or through a plate glass security window and speaks to his visitor via a telephone. In most large jails, this type of procedure is most assuredly the rule and there is never to be physical contact between the prisoner and his visitor. This even includes a man's children, should they be allowed in, and rarely is this the privilege since visiting is usually limited to adults in the immediate family. I have seen men waiting to go to trial and not even found guilty, risk being sent to the *hole,* attempting to see their children through windows and doors that are off limits to the inmates. Yes, this prohibition continues, applicable to all inmates, even the nonsentenced man, under the umbrella ruling that it is necessary for the security of the institution.

It is important to realize that the reformatory houses inmates who are viewed as graduates of the lesser correctional institutions such as detention centers and training schools. These inmates take with them all they have learned about aggression which is further expanded by the more aggressive system inherent in the reformatory. Only here, all conditions exacerbate sexual attacks even more.

Many of those confined in reformatories are recidivists, which are those who have been convicted of a crime in the past and served a sentence, were released to society, only to be returned to the institution as a parole violator or for a new crime.[19] These inmates have established reputations as jocker or punk that they are expected to uphold by the other

---

[19] The forecast is that the numbers confined in these institutions for young adults will escalate in the coming years as a result of the failure of existing programs and institutions to prevent large scale occurrences of deviant behavior. Eiji Amemiya, "The Delinquent Subculture: Population and Projections," in Paul Graubard, *Children Against Schools* (Chicago, Follett Educational Corporation, 1969), pp. 31-37.

inmates in the institution. Most important, the blacks committed to these reformatories know the white punks who were in the training school and exploitation and subordination can be expected to continue, only here on a much greater and more cruel scale.

Jails and reformatories are similar in that both house sentenced men, some serving many years and some a portion of a year's sentence. The jail, however, also houses men known as "bound-overs" or those waiting to go to trial. Here the most savage injustice can take place relative to sexual aggression, for those serving time have relatively nothing to lose in a sexual attack. The individual awaiting trial then becomes a victim of the victims themselves, or those already convicted and confined for a crime. Davis found this phenomena, of sexual assault on those waiting for trial, to be of epidemic proportions in his study of the jail and prison system in Philadelphia. He cites the fact that a "slender 21-year-old committed to the Philadelphia Detention Center merely for pre-sentence evaluation, had been sexually assaulted within minutes of his admission." [20]

In the reformatory, in most instances, those serving sentences of two, three, and even more years, are mixed with those who only have a year or less to serve. The latter individual has much more to lose if found guilty of an infraction of the rule since he wants to keep earning "good time," or time deducted from a sentence for good behavior, so as to get out even earlier. Therefore, he may give in to sexual threats so as not to suffer being implicated, probably disbelieved, and loosing time earned toward an early release. The inmate with the longer sentence is much more lax in his obedience to the rule and more sexually aggressive since he reasons that he has to spend the time in confinement anyway, thus he may as well spend it on "his terms and not theirs," and endure additional punishment should he be apprehended in an aggressive sexual act. It is clear then, that under these circumstances, tension is built into the system

---

[20] Davis, *op. cit.*, p. 8.

itself. Those serving longer sentences are willing to run the risk of taking what they want, even if what they want is another male's body.

Gagnon indicts the prison system for its failure to attack the problem of sexuality in a realistic manner when he says, "Despite evidence of progress, there still remains a major area of behavior with which prison systems have been unable to cope. This is the problem of sexual adjustment that occurs in all institutions where one sex is deprived of social or sexual access to another. It is in this area of sexuality that the prison is perhaps more limited than it is in other areas of activity, partially because society (itself) rarely provides clear guidelines for sexual behavior even outside the penal institution." [21]

Without clear guidelines the inmates of the reformatory create their own rules. It is not unusual to see black as well as white men in the prison population with makeup * or acting prissy in a manner they consider to be the stereotype of a woman. This includes lisping, using terms such as sister or dear when addressing one another, and overtly caressing each other in the presence of the other men. This particular reformatory in Connecticut had a large number of black *sissies* who were ready for sexual play any time they could get it. Some of the black inmates took advantage of this availability, but more of their time was spent victimizing the whites. For a black to have sex with another black carried far less status than a black to have sex with a white, especially a white that was forced to become a punk, thereby attesting to the superiority of the black jock. In many instances the white homosexuals caused greater problems than the black sissies, since they would vie not only for other whites who

---

[21] John H. Gagnon and William Simon, "The Social Meaning or Prison Homosexuality," *Federal Probation*, 32:23 (March, 1968).

* Makeup is derived in many fashions by the inmates. It is usually against institutional rules to wear anything that is not prescribed by a physician. However, the men attempt to get around the rule, especially the young adults inclined toward sexual promiscuity that are homosexual, by saying that the creams and other facial applications are for treatment of acne. Also, they use the blacks from matches and food and clothing dyes as makeup applications.

wanted sex, but more so with the blacks, thereby adding to and often causing racial as well as sexual friction within the institution.

The acts of sexual aggression engaged in by the blacks in these higher institutions is almost invariably used by them to let the white inmates, as well as the staff, know that they consider themselves as the dominant, not the dominated, in spite of the fact that they are locked up. It appears to become an essential ingredient to their concept of manhood to make it known that whites are the sole object of their sexual attacks in the majority of cases. In this sense, then, black aggressors resent the black homosexuals found in the reformatory as well as other institutions; they believe that black should denote power and dominance and not be identified with the sissy-like activities of many of the black homosexuals. This resentment seems to carry over into outside society when blacks are seen with other black homosexual partners.*

In one case known to this author, a white youth was the victim of black sexual aggressors while a resident of the Training School in Connecticut. When he reached eighteen and was arrested on suspicion of stealing a car, he was taken to the county jail and bound over, waiting to go to trial. It is ironic that he was sexually assaulted by the same black youths in the jail who assaulted him in the training school several years earlier.

It cannot be emphasized too strongly or too frequently that the attitudes of the black aggressors and the white victims continue from the training school into the reformatory and jail and ultimately to the prison for the "homosexual behavior of these males is essentially acted out in terms of dominant or predatory relationships (since) the aggressive males in adult prisons have been commonly recruited from boys who had experience in juvenile institutions or 'hard-rocks' in adult institutions." [22]

---

* It appears that many of the blacks who are heterosexually oriented are offended when they see black homosexuals as they believe this deletes the black image of manliness.

[22] Buffum, *op. cit.*, pp. 15-16.

What All This Means—A Possible Explanation

A white aggressor appears to seek a victim both as a person he can relate to as well as for sexual release and domination.[23] This does not appear to be the reasoning on the part of the black aggressor. By and large, the black jock looks upon his white victim purely from the standpoint of validating his masculinity or dominance. There is little to bolster the theory that he wants sex as a further tie to a more personal relationship with a white; a tie usually sought by a white jock when he takes a white male as his own. Further proof of aggression being the object of black sexual assault is the fact that few black jocks seek out other blacks as their victims. Davis found the same phenomena true in his study and reported that of 129 assaults he studied, only thirty-seven or 29 percent involved Negro aggressors and Negro victims.[24] In fact, a black aggressor rarely even takes advantage of known black homosexuals in the institution.

It appears that there are those who do not take into account the aggressive desires of the blacks when discussing Negro sexuality in institutions. Huffman is of the opinion that the Negroes practice homosexuality in a primitive manner, according to stimulus and response, and accept a man when a woman is not available.[25] He goes on to say that "they appear to have no feelings of recrimination or discrimination, in relation to their partners, except in so called miscegenation liaisons." [26]

Huffman does not appear to view the black man's aggression in totality; he attempts to make the black man appear primitive and ape-like where in fact the exact opposite is true. The blacks control themselves in quite a sophisticated manner; they prefer men because men are available to dominate thereby elevating the black man's self-image, or so he believes. Also the blacks do have feelings toward their

---

[23] *Ibid.*, p. 23.

[24] Davis, *op. cit.*, p. 15.

[25] Arthur V. Huffman, "Sex Deprivation in a Prison Community," *Journal Of Social Therapy*, 6:180 (1960).

[26] *Ibid.*

partners, and the predominant feeling is that the partner must be a white. Therefore, miscegenated liaisons are the preferred union as seen by the black jock. Davis has shown that the blacks on their way to trial in the sheriff's van took advantage of a white youth.[27] How long could they have been deprived of a woman, yet they sought out a white male for their aggressive act. They most likely would have committed the same act of aggression on a white if they caught him walking alone through Central Park.

There is some agreement with Huffman, by this author, in his observation that homosexuality is probably more prevalent among Negroes in the population of a large prison than among the white population.[28] Because of this and because blacks take whites as their victims, there is a constant catalyst for racial tension and extreme violence in penal institutions. This occurs frequently in institutions housing young offenders where tempers may be shorter and mature decisions about the repercussions of a sexual assault somewhat more lacking than in an adult prison. The white population is aware that sex is not the overbearing object of black aggression, but power is the issue. Hatred then becomes the key word and "this hatred . . . can and frequently does lead to serious racial disturbances within prisons. Single or multiple stabbings of participants in the miscegenated homosexual activities are a commonplace disorder in many of the affected institutions." [29]

Buffum is even more emphatic about the differences in black aggression versus white victimization. He states that many correctional institutions reach a parity or even a majority status relative to sheer numbers in favor of Negroes in many jails and prisons, therefore bringing the "racial conflict into the confines of the penal institution. Negro males, deprived of even more methods of validating masculinity than even the most economically depressed white males, find even greater need for continuing validation of masculinity in

---

[27] Davis, *op. cit.*, p. 12.

[28] Huffman, *op. cit.*, p. 173.

[29] *Ibid.*, p. 174.

relationships to women. In this sense the Negro male even more than the white finds continuing validation of masculinity needs in aggressive homosexual relationships in prison." [30] Evidently this sense of validation of masculinity by the blacks continues even when the youthful black inmate is released. Some of the young blacks related to this author that they rape young whites on the outside "just to show them who is the man." *

I do, however, agree with Buffman's contention that "Negro homosexuality, in general, and Negro homosexuality in prison, in particular, seem different than white experience. The Negro male is less likely to express strong positive sentiments toward homosexual experience if he has had it. It is the lack of strong positive or negative affect which characterizes Negro homosexuality both in the free community and in the prison. The motive of the Negro prisoner to have homosexual contact is more directed by dominance needs and sexual access than by strong needs for affective investment. Indeed these needs may tend to involve the Negro in prison in the aggressor role in homosexual rape more often than the white prisoner." [31] It is too simplistic to imagine that the blacks are merely seeking out whites because no women are available. Rather, I believe, as does Irwin, that underlying this aggression of the blacks "is the deep seated resentment which lower class blacks harbor against the white middle-class youth." [32] The same black aggressive behavior seems to apply to adult blacks since seventy-two of the 129 cases of sexual assault, or 56 percent of the aggression discovered by Davis in the Philadelphia correctional system were assault performed by older adult blacks on younger whites,

---

* The word man is a black colloquialism connotating the law and, even more particularly in ghetto areas, directly meaning the white man or the white law.

[30] Buffum, *op. cit.,* p. 22.

[31] Buffum, *op. cit.,* p. 22.

[32] John Irwin, "Some Research Questions on Homosexuality in Jails and Prisons" (A working paper presented to the Conference on Prison Homosexuality, 1971, p. 2, as cited in Buffum, *op. cit.,* p. 23).

and the primary goal of their behavior was to degrade their white victim by such actions.[33]

Since the scapegoat is almost always white, it has been obvious that "of all the characteristics so far examined . . . race is the single most important socio-demographic characteristic associated with victimization."[34] As these individuals continue their lives caught in a web of arrest and incarceration one truth prevails. The victim and aggressor feel ready to take their "place among the so-called 'elite of crime' as benefits his prison training in the homosexual mores of his upbringing. Be he jocker or punk, his status has inevitably preceded his coming and is well-known among the inmate body having been heralded by those he consorted with in other institutions."[35]

---

[33] Davis, *op. cit.*, p. 15.
[34] Dinitz, Miller and Bartollas, *op. cit.*, p. 9.
[35] Huffman, *op. cit.*, p. 172.

CHAPTER **5**

POWER AND VIOLENCE—AMERICA'S NATURAL MODE OF EXPRESSION

Power—The Basis of Aggression

"**P**OWER, NOT IDEAS, defines America for the rest of the world. We live in a society dominated by power;" [1] for today we glorify the power of violence while ignoring the pity of it. "Violence is ugly and in its criminal forms is the ultimate human degradation." [2] Yet, the individual, legally classified as a criminal, is the product of a society that naturally turns to violence to solve its problems. Much of our nation's violence has centered in groups struggling for power and these groups have constituted, by and large, a majority of our population. Therefore, because this majority has benefited from the "economic structure of the nation, they have been conservative, and determined to hold what they have. They have repeatedly seen attempts to partake of that success by those excluded—the poor, the blacks, the ethnic minorities . . . as imperiling their own position." [3] The law, on the other hand, upholds the wishes of the dominant group, thereby placing the have nots in a position of legal as well as economic and social disadvantage.

These have nots, then, constitute a subculture of people

---

[1] Michael Harrington, *The American Character* (Santa Barbara, The Center for Study of Democratic Institutions, Fund For The Republic, 1971), p. 7.

[2] Ramsey Clark, *Crime In America* (New York, Pocket Books 1971), pp. 323-324.

[3] Michael Wallace, "The Uses Of Violence in American History," *American Scholar*, 40:99 (Winter, 1971).

"who are disaffected, jaded or needy (and) will more readily than the 'respectable' groups sanction the mastery of the environment through criminal and violent means." [4] It is possible then, to view violence as a result of a significant segment of the population as suffering from feelings of "relative deprivation and from straight forward deprivation." [5]

Violence therefore is not peculiar to individuals alone, rather it can and usually does reflect the feelings of a significant segment of the population. "While legal systems deal with the individual as a unit of guilt and innocence, it is really the group which is at the heart of all but a small proportion of criminal proceedings . . . Of course, any group based concept of guilt would contradict fundamental Judeo-Christian notions of personality and rectitude, and involve racist, caste-like, or nationalistic rather than universalistic criteria for the administration of justice." [6] Yet, this is precisely the issue, the origins of violence are seen in the attitude of the majority relative to race and nationality, as well as the social and economic status of those considered to belong to that segment of society more generally classified as disadvantaged. In a reverse role, many of those who are arrested and incarcerated look upon the State, and therefore the majority, as acting violently and unfairly toward them as a group, since as the minority, they have little to say in the making of the very law under which they are punished when it is violated.

Relating Violence and Sexual Assaults in Prison

The sexual assaults that occur within prisons and jails cannot be categorized as homosexual attacks, rather they are assaults by heterosexually-oriented males on other males for political reasons, i.e. in order to show power or dominance over other human beings. Sexual release for these attackers is also a definite factor in their behavior, but "it appears that the need for sexual release is not the primary motive for

---

[4] Lionel Tiger, *Men In Groups* (New York, Vintage Books, 1970), p. 221.
[5] *Ibid.*
[6] *Ibid.*, p. 223.

sexual aggression . . . (for) in a sexually segregated population, autoeroticism would seem a much easier and more
'normal' method of release than homosexual rape." [7]

It is also of consequence that those "who commit perver-
sions in prison are neither psychotic, intellectually defective,
nor sexually dangerous persons, (nor do they) become
involved, presumably because of mental disorders or intel-
lectual inability to comprehend the seriousness of their
actions." [8] More precisely, "institutional behavior rarely
arises *sui generis*. It is only in the complex interaction between the pre-institutional experience of inmates and staff,
and in the institutional structure that an adequate picture
of the final mixture may be formed.[9] The obvious fact is
that victimization, degradation, racism and humiliation of
the victims are the foremost reasons why assaults are perpetrated upon men in this setting. Thus, the release of sexual
tension is but a cover for the "social and psychological meaning that such release has and the motives and beliefs that is
expresses for him (the inmate). The source of this set of
values does not reside in the prison experience, but outside
the prison in the community at large." [10]

The Powerless Poor—The Origins of the Inmate Population

It has been said that "violence, all violence, is both sexual and political in character, and that its explanation lies
in the psychosexual disfigurement of the young male. Violence in the United States is indisputedly synonymous with
young male aggression, murder, rape, assault, (and) gratuitous brutality. Acts of violence by young men are political
acts in the specific sense that they are long delayed reactions
against authority, against powerlessness before authority,

---

[7] Alan J. Davis, "Sexual Assaults in the Philadelphia Prison System and
Sheriff's Vans," *Transaction Magazine*, 6:15 (1968).

[8] Arthur V. Huffman, "Sex Deprivation in a Prison Community," *The
Journal Of Social Therapy*, 6:181 (1960).

[9] Peter C. Buffum, *Homosexuality in Prisons* (Washington, D.C., National
Institute of Law Enforcement and Criminal Justice, U.S. Government Printing
Office, February, 1972), p. 8.

[10] *Ibid.*, p. 9.

authority usually presented to males in boyhood in the person of the dominant woman." [11]

Primarily, the sense of powerlessness felt by many of the inmates causes them to take out this deprivation in violent actions upon others. Ramsey Clark has stated that there are millions of powerless people in America.[12] A person is powerless when he is black, or white from the disadvantaged class and cannot find employment because of his color or because he lives in the inner city bereft of the many services available to the average middle-class citizen.

The result is that "powerless people live by their wits. For them, rules of society are alien in spirit and in fact. The law is irrelevant . . . because you have no rights and you have no power. Those who have no rights will, given time, not respect the rights of others. Crime will exist while people do not respect the rights of others." [13] A significant portion of our population, about forty million Americans, see violence as the only answer to their condition. They are from the disadvantaged sector of our society, from places of extreme poverty from which four in five of all serious crimes flow. "It is here that the clear connection between crime and the harvest of poverty, discrimination, segregation . . . and injustice is manifest." [14] We know that of "the 1.2 million criminal offenses handled each day by some part of the United States correctional system, 80 percent are members of the lowest 12 percent income group—or black and poor." [15]

The results of these statistics are horribly brought home to the other classes in America that do not share this climate of deprivation for "it is the crimes of the poor and powerless people that most enrage and frighten the affluent, comfortable and advantaged majority. Riots, muggings, robbery, and rape

[11] Doston Rader, "The Sexual Nature of Violence," *New York Times*, October 22, 1973, p. C-31.

[12] Clark, *op. cit.*, p. 226.

[13] *Ibid.*, pp. 227, 230.

[14] Clark, *op. cit.*, pp. 40-41.

[15] Jessica Mitford, *Kind and Unusual Punishment* (New York, Alfred A. Knopf, 1971), p. 289.

are loathsome not only because they are inherently irrational and inhumane but because they and their causes are so foreign to the experience of people with power, that they are incomprehensible." [16]

Inmate Profile—A Key to Understanding Sexual Aggression

With an understanding of the life-style of the normal inmate, it is possible to comprehend some of the reasons why the incarcerated individuals are aggressive, and more important, why many of them seek sexual domination of other men to express this aggressive behavior. "Male prison populations are not random selections from larger society and do not reflect the usual distributions of the population in terms of education, income, ethnicity, occupation, social class and general life-style . . . they tend to be drawn from deprived sections of the society or from families imbedded in what we have come to call the culture of poverty." [17] Even more tragically, it has become known that the slums are producing the highest rate of crime, vice, and financial dependence. They are sites of physical deprivation, spiritual despair and breeding grounds for cynicism. The families are failing, the schools are failing and society is failing the slum youth.[18]

The result of this horrendous condition is that we have a society within a society. A dual struggle of a society outside the walls attempting to cut itself off from those behind bars, when in reality the deprivations suffered by the inmate is, in many instances, a direct result of the obvious contradictions found in free society itself. In the area of education alone, over 30 percent of the population above twenty-five years of age have twelve or more years of education. Only 10 percent of the inmates have this much schooling. Vocationally, 15 percent of the male work force have a profes-

---

[16] Clark, *op. cit.*, p. 21.

[17] John H. Gagnon and William Simon, "The Social Meaning Of Prison Homosexuality," *Federal Probation*, 32:24 (March, 1968).

[18] *Juvenile Delinquency and Youth Crime*, Task Force Report, President's Commission on Law Enforcement and Administration of Justice, U.S. Government Printing Office, Washington, D.C., 1967), pp. 42-43.

sion, while one fourth of 1 percent of the inmates are in this group. Half of the inmates are unskilled laborers, and only 20 percent of the state labor force is engaged in unskilled labor.[19]

With this type of background it is clear that "many coming to prison are so disorganized, so confused and so lacking in self-control that they cannot focus on any one subject for more than a few minutes. Born in bedlam, physically abused in infancy and childhood, they have lived amid chronic violence, fear, and confusion." [20]

The Black Poor—Conditions Leading to Aggression

Ramsey Clark states that there is a dangerous risk in America today that may cause us to misinterpret the crime picture among the blacks. More cogently he says, "crime flows clearly and directly from the brutalization and dehumanization of racism, poverty and injustice . . . There is nothing inherent in black character that causes crime. On the contrary, the slow destruction of human dignity caused by white racism is responsible. This is the most pitiable result of this huge wrong of the American people." [21] It is this dehumanization that results in a feeling that is even worse than prejudice, and that is the sense of powerlessness among the blacks.[22]

The rampant type of racism that is dominant in America is not merely a social cliche, rather it is at the very root of the sexual assaults perpetrated by black men on white victims in prison and in jail. Not only are the blacks subject to discrimination in society, but it is a simple fact that black men are victimized by crime and subjected to arrest entirely

---

[19] "National Profile Of Correction," *Correction in the U.S. Crime and Delinquency* (Washington, D.C., National Council on Crime and Delinquency, January, 1967), pp. 229-260. (Seven hundred inmates were compared with educational and occupational distribution for the state as indicated in the U.S. Census of 1960.)

[20] Clark, *op. cit.*, p. 207.

[21] *Ibid.*, p. 35.

[22] Allen D. Grimshaw, *Racial Violence in the U.S.* (Chicago, Aldine Publishing, 1969), p. 14.

out of proportion to their numbers in the population. Over 27 percent of those who are arrested are black, although blacks constitute only 11 percent of the total population. In short, two thirds of the arrests that take place occur among 2 percent of the nation's population.[23] Malcom X stated quite clearly the feelings of those blacks who find themselves incarcerated when he said, "black men are in prison in far greater numbers than their proportion in the population." [24] This fact plays no small part in the fact that the black man seeks to even the score against his white oppressors once behind the walls. He does this in part through sexual aggression. Yet, there are conditions in society that aggravate and act as a catalyst toward the aggressive behavior chosen by blacks in prison.

Racism—As the Blacks See it on the Outside

The indictment against society on behalf of the black man need not necessarily be forthcoming from the black man himself. United States District Court Judge A. Leon Higginbothan Jr., stated that our Constitution itself was in part a racist document; "we will never be able to communicate with the black men in our prisons today unless we face the fact that racism continues in contemporary society . . . and we will not be able to solve today's racial problems either in our prisons or on the outside merely by suggesting that some of the black men who are angry are a few isolated hard core militants." [25] The tragic fact for the black man is that "by and large our prisons are reserved for those with dark skins, little money, or unconventional life styles." [26]

The racism that is rampant is known to the poor blacks. It is a technique meant to "keep black people on the bot-

---

[23] Congressman John Conyers, Jr., "The Criminal Justice System," *Congressional Record* (House), vol. 119, no. 29, February 22, 1973), p. H-1102.

[24] Malcom X, *The Autobiography of Malcom X* (New York, Grove Press, 1966), p. 183.

[25] The American Friends Service Committee, *Struggle for Justice: A Report on Crime and Punishment in America* (New York, Hill and Wang, 1971), p. 101.

[26] *Ibid.*

tom, arbitrarily and dictatorily, as the (racists) have done in this country for nearly 300 years." [27] The black man himself has a mission, in the face of this racism, for he is "seeking full participation in the decision making processes affecting (his life) ." [28] Yet, as the black community seeks self-determination and self-identity, they simultaneously are aware that "Negroes are more likely to be suspected of crime than are the whites. They are also more likely to be arrested and are less likely to secure bail, and so are more liable to be counted in jail statistics. They are more liable than whites to be indicted and less likely to have their cases nol prossed or otherwise dismissed. If tried, Negroes are more likely to be convicted." [29]

The theme of racism pervades the outlook of the black man inside as well as outside the walls of prison "because Negroes begin with the primary infliction of inferior racial status, (and therefore) the burdens of despair and hatred are more pervasive." [30] The poor black (like the poor white) are constantly subjected to a philosophy built on the basis of wealth and financial prosperity when in fact the black man is denied, in many instances, even the means whereby he can attempt to achieve the least material success in society. "It would be interesting to see what percentage of black men and women would be sent to prison if they were not subjected to racism and discrimination, were granted relevant education, and an equal opportunity to prosper as other American citizens, and were spared the psychological sabotage that has been directed upon their minds." [31] A signifi-

---

[27] Stokely Carmichael and Charles Hamilton, *Black Power, The Politics of Liberation in America* (New York, Vintage Books, 1967), p. 47.

[28] *Ibid.*

[29] Mitford, *op. cit.*, p. 54.

[30] Kenneth B. Clark, *Dark Ghetto* (New York, Harper and Row, 1965), p. 27.

[31] Kenneth Divons and Larry M. West, "Prison or Slavery," *The Black Scholar*, 3.6 (October, 1971); "For most minority groups . . . and most particularly the Negro, schools provide no opportunity at all for them to overcome this initial deficiency (in reading); in fact they fall farther behind the white majority in the development of several skills which are critical to making a living and participating fully in modern society." *Task Force Report: Juvenile Delinquency and Youth Crime, op. cit.*, p. 235.

cant part of this sabotage is found early in the life of a young black, "for most minority groups . . . most particularly the Negro, schools provide no opportunity at all for them to overcome this initial deficiency (reading below grade level) in fact they fall farther behind the white majority in the development of several skills which are critical to making a living and participating fully in modern society." [32]

Middle-Class Values Are Not a Way Out for the Black Inmate

The "goal of black people must not be to assimiliate into middle-class America, for that class—as a whole—is without a viable conscience as regards humanity. The values of the middle class permit the perpetuation of the ravages of the black community." [33] Yet, it is precisely the fact that "Negroes know what they want . . . but do not know how to achieve these wants." [34] In Hylan Lewis' phrase, these people are "frustrated victims of middle-class values." [35] This syndrome of seeing what one wants (in many instances needs) and not being able to obtain it, leads to the belief, on the part of a significant number of poor blacks, that they cannot possibly obtain, in a legal fashion, the goods and services available to the middle class. Poverty itself and lack of equal opportunity play a role in the attitudes that the disadvantaged black takes toward the middle class—an attitude that eventually leads to violent action on his part in many instances.

The "slum dwelling Negro's behavior stems from something deeper rooted and harder to overcome than poverty; that is the hatred of the 'man,' the white man, who seems determined to keep him in his place." [36] The result of this hatred is that the black man sees the "out of date white man . . . as offering the Negro nothing at all, except what

---

[32] *Ibid.,* p. 235.

[33] Carmichael and Hamilton, *op. cit.,* p. 40.

[34] Charles E. Silberman, *Crisis In Black and White* (New York, Random House, 1964), p. 47.

[35] *Ibid.*

[36] *Ibid.*

has always been offered the black man in society. He is saying that if the Negro wants anything further than what the
white man has always given, he is going to have to take it." [37]
What the black man is and how he feels remain the same
when he is behind bars. For as one black inmate stated,
"it is my contention that a black convict's condition in prison
or out of prison is one and the same thing. I mean the condition of the ghetto. And I mean physically and mentally
do not change when he becomes a convict." [38] The black
men behind bars, even in their rage and aggression, "are
fighting for human dignity, for empowerment, for self-
determination, for political rights—which many believe will
lead to the eventual overthrow of the system that enslaves
them." [39] Until this eventual overthrow or change occurs, the
black man in prison seeks to make the white captors imprisoned with them suffer for the discrimination he has
endured. He does this through sexual assault which he believes buttresses his status as a man, a status he is convinced is
constantly thwarted by white society and one he is willing
to die for—a concept that is part of his beliefs even when
not incarcerated.

Masculinity—The Overriding Concern of the Inmate Population

Its Affect on Sexual Aggression

The inmate has come from a segment of society where
sexuality is his claim to masculinity. Once inside the walls
he is deprived of the opposite sex upon whom, in most instances, he has centered his claim to virility. In fact "at a more
conscious level he (the inmate) may feel that his masculinity is threatened because he can see himself as a man—
in the full sense, only in a world that also contains women

---

[37] Le Roi Jones, *What Does Non-Violence Mean? Law And Resistance American Attitudes Toward Authority*, Lawrence Veysey, ed. (New York, Harper Torch, 1970), p. 189.

[38] Nicholas Horrock, "The New Breed of Convict, Black, Angry and Radical," *Newsweek Feature Service*, 23:2 (September, 1971).

[39] Mitford, *op. cit.*, p. 235.

. . . as an essential component of his self-conception, his status as a male is called into question." [40] Eventually the overly aggressive (and probably more threatened and frightened concerning his masculine image) inmate will enter into homosexual activity in which he can conceive of himself as fulfilling his masculine prowess since he will seek to control his partner which for "him and for other males in the system validate continued claims to masculine status." [41] In truth, "only sexual and physical prowess stand between them (the inmates) and a feeling of emasculation." [42]

The inmate should not be considered a unique *animal* in the frustrations he faces relative to his image of being a man, and the eventual acceptance of violence to express what he considers is his masculine image. The role of the policeman on the street and that of the correctional officer in the prison, is also based on their proving their *manhood* to the inmates. Thus, the pattern remains the same inside and outside the walls. More specifically, "as shown by their reports, the policemen feel that they have to uphold 'law and order,' and they identify this with their own individual self-esteem and masculinity. Time after time it is clear that the policeman is fighting an impotence-potency battle within himself that he extends and projects on the concept of law and order. They feel their manhood is being challenged and their reputation, on which their self-respect is based, is at stake." [43]

This struggle is not only with the adults but also with the young offenders in the community for "the black kids and the white cops—their pride, their fear, their isolation, their need to prove themselves, above all their demands for respect—are strangely alike; victims both, prisoners of an

[40] Gresham Sykes and Sheldon L. Messinger, *The Inmate Social Code and Its Functions* (New York, Social Science Research Council, Pamphlet No. 15, 1960), p. 9.

[41] Gagnon and Simon, *op. cit.,* p. 26.

[42] Davis, *op. cit.,* p. 16.

[43] Rollow May, *Power and Innocence, A Search For The Sources Of Violence* (New York, W. W. Norton, 1972), pp. 29-30.

escalating conflict they did not make and can't control." [44]
Thus what is apparent is that "almost everyone is struggling
in some form or other to build or protect his self-esteem,
and his sense of significance as a person. Both police and sus-
pects are fighting an impotency-potency battle within themselves." [45]

The importance of these observations, to this study, is
simply that the inmate sees the prison guard staff in the same
role as that of the policeman with the same struggle to dominate over him, the inmate, in a more masculine manner;
for "it appears that guards and police officers are of the
same personality type." [46] "Correctional officer candidates,
like inmates, seem to be about equal in their feelings of
aggressiveness, hostility, resentment, suspicion and desire to
act out assaultatively." [47] This similarity of feeling is known
to the inmates and they feel that they can shout out with
justification, "we don't want to be treated any longer as
statistics, as numbers, . . . we want to be treated as human
beings; we will be treated as human beings." [48]

By now it is clear that the whole *genre* of pre-institutional
and institutional behavior, both for the keepers and those
who are kept, is caught up in one orgy whereby both groups
are attempting to prove their masculinity to one another
while simultaneously seeking not to be emasculated in the
eyes of one another. The inmates' attitude toward masculinity
is inexorably bound up in his view of women and his approach toward female sexuality. To understand both is to
comprehend in large part why inmates sexually assault other
males in prison and jail.

Sexuality—The Inmates' View

We have seen that the greatest number of men that constitute the imprisoned population are drawn from the dis-

---

[44] Hans Toch, *Violent Men, An Inquiry into the Psychology of Violence*
Chicago, Aldine, 1969) , p. 49, quoted by May, *op. cit.*, p. 29.
[45] May, *op. cit.*, pp. 29-30.
[46] *Ibid.*, pp. 31-32.
[47] *Ibid.*, p. 6.
[48] *Ibid.*, pp. 31-32.

advantaged sectors of our society. It is important, therefore, to have some grasp of the meaning that normal sex plays in their lives, since sexual aggression appears to be but an extension of their feelings once behind bars.

Kinsey, as early as 1947, established certain facts that have been corroborated by even more recent studies in the field of sexuality. One of these early findings by Kinsey was that there was no "American pattern of sexual behavior as such, but rather scores of patterns could be shown to be peculiar to a particular segment of our society." [49] Yet, there is a definite finding among the disadvantaged, and therefore among those who by and large constitute the prison population. Their sexual feelings are indeed expressed differently than those who do not find themselves confined to jails and prisons.

More precisely, "men with prison histories generally have wider sexual experiences of all kinds than do men leading conventional and non-delinquent lives. These variables suggest that at the least the model male prison population enters institutions with differing commitments to sexuality than would a middle-class or working-class population." [50] The latter, or upper level male, is capable of being aroused by a variety of stimuli, whether it be thinking about females or the homosexual partner of his interest. On the other hand, the lower level male is less aroused by anything except physical contact and coitus; [51] he usually has an abundance of premarital intercourse and appears to be well versed in the homosexual culture of his neighborhood, if not taking part in it directly, then hearing first-hand accounts from his friends.

It is obvious that the actions of the inmates (in part) are a direct result of what they have experienced in the community from which they came. The same finding was apparent in the study done by Davis who found that "the principal psychological causes of sexual assaults in the

---

[49] Alfred C. Kinsey, Clyde E. Martin, and Wardell B. Pomeroy, *Sexual Behavior In The Human Male* (Philadelphia, W. B. Sanders, 1948), p. 329.

[50] Buffum, *op. cit.,* p. 9.

[51] Kinsey, *et al., op. cit.,* p. 363.

Philadelphia prison system are deeply rooted in the community in that millions of Americans are deprived of any effective way of achieving masculine self-identification through avenues other than physical aggression and sex. They belong to a class of men who rarely have meaningful work, successful families, or opportunities for constructive emotional expression and individual creativity. Therefore . . . the pathology at the root of sexual assaults will not be eliminated until fundamental changes are made in the outside community." [52] The inmates' view of sexuality is linked with the role that women have in his life, for ultimately the sexual aggressor defines his victim in female terms.

The Inmates' View of Women—How This Affects Sexual Aggression

A significant portion of lower class males are raised in homes where a female is the predominant member since there is usually a consistent lack of a male or father image in the home situation. The result is that the males in this situation seek to express themselves in ways they consider to be masculine beyond question. This includes "possession of strength and endurance and athletic skills . . . and a conceptualization of women as conquest objects." [53] Also they tend to view upper class males or "upwardly mobile peers as . . . fags or queers," [54] placing them in a female category through the use of such language since it connotes softness or frills which they identify with femininity. Kate Millett puts the role of the woman in a most dramatic perspective (one that appears to apply to the manner in which the individuals we are speaking of view women) when she says, "all the mechanisms of human inequality arose out of the foundations of male supremacy and the subjection of women, sexual politics serving historically as the foundation of all other social, political, and economic structures . . . the

---

[52] Davis, *op. cit.*, p. 16.

[53] Donald R. Cressey and David A. Ward, *Delinquency, Crime and the Social Process* (New York, Harper and Row, 1969), p. 336.

[54] *Ibid.*, p. 337

subjection of women (being) of course far more than an economic or even a political event, but a total social and psychological phenomena, a way of life." [55]

D. H. Lawrence defined power as the ability to dominate a woman and "later he applied the idea to other political situations, extending the notion of Herrschaft (defined by Max Weber as a relationship of dominance and subordination) to inferior males mastered by a superior male (for) lesser men must be seen as females." [56] This is precisely the attitude taken by the sexual aggressor in prison, relating his victim to his conception of a woman over whom he is lord and master.

Jean Genet sheds further light on the inmates' view of the weaker prisoners being seen in the role of women in prison sexuality. He himself was imprisoned at an early age in Mettray and because he was not able to defend himself against sexual attacks of the larger boys, he had to assume what he considered the passive role—the role of a woman in the sexual gratification sought by the more powerful inmates.[57] It is from Genet that one can gather a more precise meaning into black domination of whites, and more important why the black inmate seeks sodomy as the price that the white man must pay as an outward sign of the black man's superiority.

In the play *The Blacks,* Genet suggests that the white man has presented his woman to the blacks as a sort of coveted prize that he tempts the black man to take at the expense of prison and even death. "Meanwhile the black woman is imprisoned as her master's whore . . . For the white distorts love and sexuality in his subjects, forcing the black male to accept both the white woman's beauty, and scorn of the black woman." [58] Genet is bringing into focus some of the reasons why black men will treat white inmates as women;

---

[55] Millett, *Sexual Politics* (New York, Avon Books, 1970), p. 168.

[56] *Ibid.,* pp. 355-356.

[57] *Ibid.,* pp. 440-472. (Millett's account of Genet's feelings toward sexual aggression in prison.)

[58] *Ibid.,* p. 464.

for the white man has in reality divided the blacks, on the one hand holding up white women as the ideal for the black man to attain (sexually) while simultaneously placing the black woman in the role as "her masters whore (for) every brothel has its negress." [59] Thus, Genet presents the concept of woman as that to be used by the male for whatever purposes he sees fit, in any way he sees fit, and at any time he sees fit. "Masculine and feminine stand out as terms of praise and blame, authority and servitude, high and low, master and slave." [60]

Patricia Robinson buttresses the feelings that Genet has put forth about black women being used as a tool by both white as well as black men. She believes that "black women have always been told (by) black men that they are black, ugly, evil bitches, and whores—in other words, we were the real niggers in this society oppressed by whites, male and female, and the black man too." [61] It becomes more clear then that the black man is seeking to revenge himself for what he blames the white man has done to his masculine image. On the one hand the white man has held up his white woman as the coveted prize to the black man, while simultaneously making the black man put his black woman in a role even less than second rate to that of the white woman. Thus, when the black man in prison makes a white submit to sexual acts, he is saying by this action that he is in reality placing the white man in the role of his white woman and thereby obtaining the "prize"—a white woman, the prize held up to the blacks by white society itself.

This type of thinking on the part of the black man and the role of the black woman becomes even more clear in the words of Robinson. She says that the last person on the class hierarchy is the black woman.[62] It appears that the white man

---

[59] *Ibid.*

[60] *Ibid.*, p. 449.

[61] Patricia Robinson, "Poor Black Women, A Collective Statement," in *Masculine and Feminine, Readings In Sexual Mythology and Liberation of Women,* Theodore Rozack and Betty Rozack eds. (New York, Harper and Row, 1969), p, 212.

[62] *Ibid.*, p. 209.

has his way with both the white as well as the black female and the black man believed that the black female enjoyed her role belonging to the white man. The black man, more especially the black inmate, is retaliating for years of this type of domination by the white man over *his woman.*

In the arena of female assault, it has been said that "this type of callow method of shifting racial to sexual grudge and repaying injustice upon the aggressor's 'woman' is the inspiration for Eldridge Cleaver's career as a rapist. By the most depressing racist logic, Cleaver first served his apprenticeship by assaulting women of his own race, content to mimic that staggering contempt white patriarchy habitually reserves for the black female." [63] The fact is, however, and Genet makes this point quite lucid, the white man has made sexuality a political tool. The black players in Genet's play *The Blacks* have recreated a murder of a white woman for the pleasure of the all white audience (portrayed by one white guest). When the catafalque is uncovered, there is no body to behold and the white audience is shocked and angry, "for you kill us without killing us they shout." [64] Genet was not investigating the fact of racial or sexual violence, but the psychic basis of racial-sexual beliefs, exposing them as the myths of a political system.[65] However, this political system is based on sexual domination and "sexual dominion obtains nevertheless as perhaps the most pervasive ideology of our culture and provides its most fundamental concept of power." [66]

It is precisely this concept of power, seen in sexual terms, that Genet presents in the *Thief's Journal.* In the book Armand has associated "sexuality with power, with his solitary pleasure, and with the pain and humiliation of his partner . . . intercourse is an assertion of mastery, one that announces his own higher caste and proves it upon a victim

[63] Millett, *op. cit.,* p. 426 (n. 75).

[64] *Ibid.,* p. 379.

[65] *Ibid.*

[66] *Ibid.,* p. 45.

who is expected to surrender, serve and be satisfied." [67] This is the attitude that prevails in prison during sexual attacks. Genet is saying that "unless we go to the very center of the sexual politic and its sick delirium of power and violence, all our efforts at liberation will only land us again in the same primordial stews." [68] What is crucial to this study is that Genet presents, with utter frankness, the "painstaking exegisis of the barbarian vassalage of the sexual orders, the power structure of 'masculine and feminine' as revealed by a homosexual criminal world (that) mimics with brutal frankness the bourgeois heterosexual society." [69]

Black Validation of His Masculinity

We have seen that the ghetto is the incubator for crime and that it is sending more men to prison than perhaps any other factor pertinent to incarceration. "In the American Negro ghetto . . . a male is usually expected to defend . . . his race . . . or his masculinity (and) quick resort to physical combat as a measure of daring, courage, or defense of status appears to be a cultural expression." [70] It is ironic to note that the black men in the ghetto street as well as in prison are constantly testing their masculinity even in their recreation activities. There is a game called "dozens" that is played by the inmate on the street as well as inside the prison. Antagonist and protagonist seek to impugn each other's sex, wife, mother, girl friend, male lover, or masculinity, seeking to get the other to loose his temper and engage in physical combat. Often times one of the players will allude to the other's homosexual encounters with younger inmates in the prison, a slur that usually causes the accused to defend his manhood by fighting. This is all part of a violence game whereby "members of the subculture perceive themselves as aggressive; they see opportunities for violence

---

[67] *Ibid.,* p. 38.

[68] *Ibid.,* p. 42.

[69] *Ibid.,* p. 37.

[70] Hans Toch, *Violent Men, An Inquiry Into The Psychology Of Violence* (Chicago, Aldine Publishing, 1969), p. 191.

in the world around them, and they play stereotyped vio-
lence-prone games." [71] As we have seen in the previous chapter, the black prisoner is more likely to seek out homosexual
contact because of dominance [72] needs rather than sexual
relief, and it appears that the black inmate is more prone
to this type of baiting and aggression than the white inmates.

This type of aggressive behavior is not without its historical
motivation. "Because in America sex is like business advance-
ment, a prime criteria of success and hence of personal worth,
it is in sexual behavior that the damage to Negro adults shows
up in especially poignant and tragic clarity." [73] Blacks have
observed since the time of slavery that the white man has
treated black as inferior, even in his sexual relationships
with his (black) women. "The ironic fact has been that given
the inferiority of their racial status, Negro males have had
to struggle simply to believe themselves men." [74] With these
various factors (sexual, political, racial, economic) it is obvious to acknowledge that at the least there are reasons why
the black inmate seeks to dominate the white inmate in a
sexual manner; it is simply his way of asserting his masculinity while simultaneously humiliating and retaliating
against a 'historical white image' that the black man car-
ries within himself. It is true that in the final analysis "the
deprivations of imprisonment in themselves are not sufficient
to account for the form that the inmate social culture assumes
in the male and female communities. Rather, general features
of American society with respect to the cultural definition and
content of male and female roles are brought into the prison
setting and function to determine the direction and focus
of the inmate cultural systems." [75]

The direction that the aggression itself takes, in relation
to the type of sexual act performed on the victim, is impor-

---

[71] *Ibid.*

[72] See Chapter 4 of this volume.

[73] Kenneth B. Clark, *op. cit.,* p. 67.

[74] *Ibid.,* pp. 17-18

[75] Stanton Wheeler, "Socialization in Correctional Institutions," *Crime and
Justice,* Vol. 3, Leon Radzinowicz and Marvin E. Wolfgang eds., (New York,
Basic Books, 1971), p. 114.

tant to this study since it portrays the method in which the aggressor seeks to make himself appear as the dominant figure (male) and the victim appear as the dominated (female). The choice of forced sexuality chosen to achieve this end is almost invariably the act of sodomy: the aggressor believing this to be the most humiliating role for the victim to be forced to accept as his fate.

Sodomy—Its Role in Inmate Sexual Aggression

The ordinary citizen who has little or no contact with jails or prison life, save that which is essentially written about sexual attack or death that makes the headlines, is shocked to learn that perverted acts are common in prison life. Yet, the public attempts to ignore the fact that the act of sexual domination and subjugation occurs even in the initiation rites of young pledges (their) sons into certain fraternities. Once more, the rites involve definite sodomistic acts which are usually not carried out in actuality but are present nevertheless. One such fraternity makes the pledges strip naked, then bend over after having greased a nail which is handed to a senior member of the fraternity standing behind them. Although the nail is never delivered to the buttocks, the pledge gets the idea that he has subjected himself to another male in this manner.[76] The inmate in prison, chosen as the victim, is not so lucky. The attacker not only makes sure he completes the act of sodomy, but usually invites his friends to share his punk, thereby making the act even more humiliating and "demaling" for the victim.

In a cogent and indicting statement Millett says that "although 'straight' society may be affronted at the thought, homosexual art is by no means without insights into heterosexual life, out of whose milieu it grows and whose notions it must, perforce, imitate and repeat, even parody." [77] She is of course stressing the idea that the homosexual encounter involves the act of domination and subjugation for the vic-

---

[76] Tiger, *op. cit.*, p. 187-188.

[77] Millett, *op. cit.*, p. 447.

tim, as it does for many females who have intercourse with heterosexually oriented males.

Genet's first-hand experiences as an inmate appear to support Millet's contentions since Genet says that in prison the "sex role is established once and for all at two polarities of inferior and superior . . . masculine is superior strength, feminine is inferior weakness." [78] In his novel *Our Lady Of The Flowers* Genet captures the political heart of sodomy as the preferred mode of sexual dominance when the character, Darling, who is buggering Divine, says, "a male who fucks a male is a double male." [79] This is precisely the attitude taken by the sexual aggressor in prison. It has been said that "it has been fashionable for some time to visit the white man's sins on his woman," [80] and the aggressor in prison makes the male victim exactly that—a woman for political reasons of showing his power over such an individual for "it is interesting that male victims of rape at the hands of other males often feel twice imposed upon, as they have not only been subjected to forcible and painful intercourse, but further abused in being reduced to the status of a female." [81]

Norman Mailer appears to support Millett's viewpoint about the political ramifications of sexuality in the heterosexual sense. He believes that "a rapist is a rapist only to the 'square,' to the superior perception of Hip, rape is a 'part of life' and should be assessed by the subtly critical method based on whether the act possesses 'artistry' or real desire." [82] In his play *The American Dream,* "sodomy has a number of possible meanings in Rojack's mind (and) homosexuality . . . a forbidden species of sexuality at which he is an expert and over which he holds copyright; or anal rape, which is his way of expressing contemptuous mastery." [83] Even Sartre characterized this "sex act as the festival of

[78] *Ibid.*, p. 445.

[79] *Ibid.*

[80] *Ibid.*, pp. 378-379.

[81] *Ibid.*, p. 70, n. 50.

[82] *Ibid.*, p. 416.

[83] *Ibid.*, p. 29.

submission, also the ritual renewal of the feudal contract whereby the vassal became the lord's liegeman." [84] Therefore, the aggressor in prison is certainly not alone in viewing this act as uniquely his, or his own special invention.

Millett claims that the characters in Mailer's stories who perform such acts as anal intercourse are merely attempting to cover their homosexuality by extra masculine testimony and actions. Yet, and here is the heart of most of the sexual dominance in prison and jail as expressed by Genet, the victim forced into such an act does not want to see himself or have others see him "to be faggot, damned, leprous—to cease to be virile were either to cease to be—or to become the most grotesque form of feminine inferiority—queer." [85] Again, even Genet sees submission to an attacker as a grotesque form of femininity. The fact that he, as well as the aggressors, have their own most often erroneous definition of femininity does not prevent them from seeing the one who is made to submit taking the role of a woman.

D. J. Jethron, in Mailer's *Why We Are in Vietnam,* seems to add the final note on this subject of anal intercourse for Jethron boastfully confirms that "buggery confers an extra honor on the 'male' partner conquering a potential equal, 'cause asshole is harder to enter than cunt and so reserved for the special tool,' to be buggered is to be hopelessly humiliated." [86] Because in the attacker's mind, it reduces the victim to the political role of a female, submission to a greater power. The black man in prison takes up the same reasoning in his attacks on white victims.

Black Attitudes Toward Rape

D. H. Lawrence in *The Woman Who Rode Away* depicts a white woman as being captured by dark-skinned males. The captive is humiliated, raped, beaten, tortured, and finally stripped and murdered. But, as the story line goes, what can one expect of savages "since we all know how they

---

[84] *Ibid.,* p. 446.
[85] *Ibid.,* p. 434.
[86] *Ibid.,* p. 437.

treat their women." [87] The comment itself is revealing since it shows "that the office of sexual avenger is of course left in the hands of the dark male." [88] "The very pattern of the tale cleverly provides satisfaction for the white males' guilt feelings over the dark people and 'primitives' whom he exploits. He will atone for whatever injustice he has brought to them by throwing them his woman to butcher, advancing his dominion over her in the process, and substituting his own rival as the scapegoat for imperialist excesses." [89] This account appears to sum up, although in a somewhat literary manner, the feeling of a significant number of men toward women in our society. The tragic aftermath of this type of thinking, on the part of both white and black members of society, is simply that many black men seek to fulfill the white man's hidden feelings toward 'his women.' When the white woman is not available for these political reasons, the black aggressor simply substitutes the white male for the same role.

Thus, the heart of sexual domination in prison is exposed when one begins to realize that "as white racist ideology is exposed and begins to erode, racism's older protective attitudes toward (white) women also begins to give way. And priorities of maintaining male supremacy might outweigh even those of white supremacy; sexism may be more endemic in our own society than racism." [90] Yet, we cannot turn to a theory of sexual needs for the aggression occurring in our prisons for we have seen that power and degradation are the primary reasons for attack on weaker men. The politico-sexual activity of the inmate is bound up in his concept of women and "it is the location of homosexual behavior on continua of activity-passivity, masculinity-femininity and aggression-submission that defines the 'normality' of the adjustment. The homosexual behavior of these males is essentially

[87] Millett, *op. cit.*, p. 377.

[88] *Ibid.*, p. 378.

[89] *Ibid.*

[90] *Ibid.*, p. 63.

acted out in terms of dominant or predatory relationships." [91]

Billy Robinson, a black inmate serving a sentence in the
Cook County Jail in Chicago, is said to be a "powerful and
political writer in the tradition of Eldridge Cleaver and
George Jackson." [92] So his opinions about the black man's
attitude toward sex and aggression appears to be rather
important to this study. He admittedly had trouble solving
the masculinity message he claims was embedded in Cleaver's
writings, but, of one thing he appears to be quite certain; the
white man must pay, and pay through sexual assault, for the
injustices that the black man has had to endure. He himself
states quite lucidly how this repayment is to be extracted
from the victims. He asked "the question that bugged me
'did the possibility of my continued existence preclude the
possibility of my being a 'man'? If I, if we, were men, why
did we accept this bullshit (that of the white man) like a
bunch of bitches?" [93] He continues, "in prison, the the black
dudes have a little masculinity game they play. It has no
name, really, although I call it whump of fuck a white boy—
especially the white gangsters or syndicate men, the bad juice
boys, the hit men, et cetera. The black dudes go out of their
way to make faggots out of them. And I know that by and far,
the white cats are faggots. They will drop their pants and
bend over and touch their toes and get had before they will
fight. So, knowing this, what kind of men did this make us?" [94]
He continues, trying to find the reason why he uses sex as a
manifestation of his masculinity, and in so doing, questions
his actions shedding further light on the act of sodomy. He
says, "I knew deep down in my bones, that if we let them
rape our women and lynch our brothers and run our lives
without dying in an attempt to stop it, we men, all of us,
had carried touch-your-toe faggotism two or three steps

[91] Buffum, *op. cit.*, p. 15.
[92] Divons and West, *op. cit.*, p. 28.
[93] *Ibid.*, p. 29.
[94] *Ibid.*

further than they." [95] Again, the constant refrain of sodomy, the constant reminder that to reduce a male to the status of a female by forcible rape was the single most dominating thing for the black man, and the most humiliating part for the white inmate. In the outside females fulfill this role through the act of coitus. In prison it is only fulfilled for men through creating a surrogate heterosexual relationship.

Some Basic Facts About Why the Black Man is Bitter

We have seen the black man's reaction to his white fellow inmates, but, it is necessary to cite one instance that may provide the reader with the facts upon which some of the blacks base their aggressive tendencies, and these arise from the prison itself.

A letter smuggled out of Soledad Prison gives some idea of what the prison setting can be like:

> Never more than 6 blacks were allowed on max row, which houses 24 inmates. Thus, the remaining 18 cells were occupied by anti-black Caucasian and Mexican inmates who race talk us in shifts so that its done 24 hours a day. On their exercise periods they spit, throw urine, and feces into our cells while the officials stand by in indifference and approval. They, the officials, call us hammers and niggers too . . . The prison officials here stopped serving the meals and deliberately selected the Caucasian and Mexican inmates . . . to serve the meals and they immediately proceeded to poison our meals by filling food to be issued to us with cleanser powder, crushed up glass, spit, urine, and feces while the officials stood by and laughed." [96]

What actions such as these showed is simply that "residual racial practices surviving from the era of slavery show that discrimination is not simply a matter of intentional policy; it also emerges from deeply ingrained attitudes and institutional prejudices that still survive." [97] In most instances as

---

[95] *Ibid.*

[96] The American Friends Service Committee, *Struggle for Justice: A Report on Crime and Punishment in America* (New York, Hill and Wang, 1971), p. 110.

[97] *Ibid.*, p. 109.

conditions now exist "the justice system functions to maintain racist relationships between the white majority and the black, brown, red, and yellow minorities in America. The command obedience structure of racism has existed in the criminal justice system since the settlement of this country." [98]

We as a people may finally come to realize that "perhaps we make the first step of the long hard journey ahead by our honesty and willingness to admit that our nation has caused much rage, that our nation has often been grossly unjust in the treatment of blacks and that we may have an obligation to work swiftly to eradicate the many consequences of the injustice rather than keep pretending that the problem never existed." [99]

---

[98] *Ibid.,* p. 107.
[99] *Ibid.,* p. 101.

CHAPTER **6**

WHAT ALL THIS MEANS—CAN ANYTHING BE DONE TO AFFECT CHANGE?

IT IS OBVIOUS that something is radically wrong within our jails, prisons, and reformatories, but also within the community as well since it is ultimately responsible for the attitudes and actions of those who find themselves incarcerated. A partial answer to such violence may well be that the present concept of justice is simply too nebulous for current judicial and social change to affect it, and this failure may rest on the fact that society fails to recognize that criminal justice is dependent upon social justice. Yet, the concept of justice, as seen in our criminal law, evidently is a kaleidoscope that has no special focus since:

> to blacks and other minorities, criminal law may appear as an instrument of oppression; to the poor, a barrier to perpetuate an unjust status quo; to the young, a coercer of conformity to middle-aged, middle-class, Puritan virtues; to mid-America, a front line defense against anarchy; to legal theorists, a delicate balancing of individual and social obligations; to politicians, an expedient means of relieving pressures to "do something" about politically insoluble problems; to social scientists, a power clash among competing interest groups; to moralists, a reaffirmation of the community's ethical values; to psychiatrists, a quasi-religious ritual that relieves the tension of moral conflict among law-abiding citizens; and to missionaries of all persuasions, a challenge to reform those who, whether from illness or perversity, have strayed from the straight path.[1]

[1] American Friends Service Committee, *Struggle for Justice: A Report on Crime and Punishment in Amercia* (New York, Hill and Wang, 1971), p. 10.

92

The clear fact is that every sector of society has a clear stake in justice and every aspect of society pays when injustice is done, even to the most 'obscure citizen.' Therefore, any attempt to suggest alternatives, relative to corrections itself, must be seen and weighed in the larger context of the whole of society. In a more specific sense, before suggestions for change can be offered, it is necessary for the citizens to realize that they are responsible for the changes that must occur, for:

> the community outside the prison walls must never separate itself from the community inside the jailhouse. And the corrective measures against crime must be at the least partially administered in the community. The essential problem is not that of an 'improper' individual behind bars; for most of us sense intuitively that the problem basically is that of an improper society outside the gates. It is a society that is rampant with inherent contradictions.[2]

The Philosophical Approach—Changing the System Itself

Among the most needed changes is that "eventually we will have to shift away from dealing with the crime to dealing with the individual who committed the crime on the basis of his psychological makeup. To do this will require considerable reeducation of legal and judicial institutions as well as the public itself." [3]

A sound beginning toward this necessary change must be made with the public changing their present view of the offender himself. "It is clear that our present attitudes toward criminals are characterized by a refusal to grant them the benefit of possessing human qualities." [4] The effect of this lack of understanding, in reality a lack of education, is felt

---

[2] Congressman John Conyers, Jr., "The Criminal Justice System," *Congressional Record* (House), vol. 119, no. 29, February 22, 1973, p. H-1102.

[3] Daniel C. Jordan and Larry Dye, *Delinquency As Assessment of the Juvenile Delinquency Act of 1968* (Amherst, University of Massachusetts, 1970), p. 24.

[4] Denis Zabo, "Do Prisons Have A Future" in *The Future of Imprisonment in a Free Society*, Vol. 2 (Chicago, St. Leonard House, 1965), p. 73.

by the accused in confinement. Society merely desires "that inmates . . . be kept securely caged, and those who wish to maintain their employment must take heed of this mandate. Most prison employees, in fact, share the public delusion growing out of the convict bogery and heartily devote themselves to its implementation." [5]

Admittedly, the task of reeducation and reorientation of the public's attitude, and eventually of the judicial system itself, is difficult but necessary if conditions are to be reversed. The inmate seeking to prove his dominance is in reality acting out a feeling of vengeance that has its roots in a distant past, yet a past that still affects the aggressors' actions within the present penal setting. "Centuries before vengeance as an admitted motive passed for general practice in the most advanced nations, it was recognized as an aggravant of crime. It caused crime. Society, in its quest for justice, sought vengeance through a major social institution, to which the people could look for leadership-government." [6] Unfortunately, society is still looking to government, the courts, and the jails to revenge itself on those who have violated the law. In turn, the inmate takes retaliatory action against the weaker inmates in the prison itself and the cycle is once again repeated. Revenge makes revenge, nothing more and nothing less.

It is never too early to begin the task of crime prevention through proper education and socialization of our children. "To prevent crime we must begin with young children of preschool and primary school years. Professionals could find 90 percent of the children likely to become delinquent. We may have to live with the rest; we do not have to live with the most. That we do tells us much about our character. It means that, knowing we create criminals, we continue. Later, frightened, we seek to control them by force." [7] So tragic is our

[5] Harry Elmer Barnes, "A Menace To Rehabilitation" in *The Future of Imprisonment in a Free Society*, Vol. 2 (Chicago, St. Leonard House, 1965), p. 12.

[6] Ramsey Clark, *Crime In America* (New York, Simon and Schuster Pocket Book edition, 1971), p. 199.

[7] *Ibid.*, p. 220.

failing to prevent crime among the young that a prominent official affiliated with Youth Services in a large eastern city believes that the way things are at present, concerning the lack of services available and the conditions of the institutions, it would be better if the young delinquents were not even detected.[8]

The pre-primary and pre-school years are crucial in the formation of positive attitudes on the part of our young children. The controversial Head Start Program has made a contribution toward bringing "about a greater social competence in disadvantaged children (that is) an individual's everyday effectiveness in dealing with his environment. A child's social competence may be described as his ability to master appropriate formal concepts, to perform well in school, to stay out of trouble with the law, and to relate well to adults and other children." [9] Dr. Edward Ziegler, former Director of the Office of Child Development, said that young people who become school dropouts, juvenile delinquents, and those who have opted for the drug culture, chose this behavior in part because of a negative self-image and "a hostility that in all too many cases has been honestly come by." [10] Head Start can help in the area of social, motivational, and emotional factors "with respect to the malaise that afflicts so many young people." [11]

The Role of the School in Crime Prevention and Aggression

The youngster who has been prepared for school by conscientious pre-primary attention must not be left to suffer negative primary and secondary school experiences that often encourage delinquency and lead to the incarceration of

---

[8] Milton Lunger, "Charles Mangel, How to Make a Criminal Out of a Child," *Look Magazine* (June 29, 1971), p. 53.

[9] Representative John Brademus, "Head Start, Success or Failure" *Congressional Record*, vol. 119, no. 148, October 4, 1973, p. E-6308. Remarks are those of Dr. Edward Ziegler, former Director of Office of Child Development within the Department of Health, Education and Welfare.

[10] *Ibid.*, p. 6309.

[11] *Ibid.*

many youngsters. Presently, and in too many instances, it is a fact that schools "are failing dismally in what has always been regarded as one of their primary tasks . . . to be the 'great equalizer of the conditions of men,' facilitating the movement of the poor and disadvantaged into the mainstream of American economic and social life. This failure is not new; it is one the United States has tolerated for over a century." [12]

Many of the "educators know far too little about those negatives (fear and violence in school, overcrowding, negative home situations) and how they affect students." [13] They know far less about the ghetto conditions in which many of their students live day to day. These conditions breed crime and lead to the incarceration of too many young men from the inner city. All too often this syndrome (rejection from school and eventual clashes with the law) can be traced to the fact that "too many young people find the formal high school program boring, irrelevant, and even uninformative." [14] In one state alone more than half of the boys committed to its juvenile detention centers are there for truancy, absenteeism, and school related problems.[15] The answer to this problem is not the dissolution of schools, but rather meaningful educational alternatives which must be offered to students to educate and interest them so as not to lead to boredom, lack of interest, and eventual conflict with themselves, their society, and the law. "Available evidence strongly suggests that delinquent commitments result in part from adverse or negative school experiences of some youth, and, further, that there are fundamental defects within the educational system, especially as it touches lower income youth, that actively contribute to these negative experiences,

---

[12] Charles E. Silberman, *Crisis In The Classroom, The Remaking of American Education* (New York, Vintage Books, 1971), pp. 53-54.

[13] Arthur Clinton, "The Half Outs," New York *Daily News*, December 16, 1971, p. 12-C.

[14] *New York Times*, July, 1971, p. 7.

[15] Larry Dye and Arthur Eve, "Deviancy: An Unknown Factor in Education" (unpublished paper, Amherst, University Massachusetts, School of Education, 1972), p. 9.

thereby increasing rather than decreasing the chances that some youth will chose the illegitimate alternatives." [16] The schools must alter their present conduct and begin to relate to all their students for "the school's power extends into the indefinite future. . . . It is as if a prison had the authority to permanently maim or cripple prisoners for disobeying rules; the schools' jurisdiction lasts only three or four years, but its sentences can last a lifetime." [17]

How the Police Affect Aggression of the Offender

We have seen that the police can do much toward aggravating situations in which juveniles find themselves, thereby leading to arrest, trial, and eventual incarceration. Often this antagonistic and "legalistic approach comes at the problem from the wrong direction. More effective laws, police, courts, and prisons . . . will not solve basic structural weaknesses that create youthful discontents." [18]

There are approximately 420,000 police in over forty thousand separate agencies throughout the nation [19] who are charged with maintaining law and order among the people. It is an established fact that many of the juveniles who come under the veil of police attention are viewed by the officers as being different from the rest of society. The officer may have a personally negative attitude toward the young men he encounters while on duty, for "many police pick up white as well as black youths merely because they do not like their walk, or perhaps their hairdo." [20] More seriously, some officers may have prejudices, which are obvious from their ar-

---

[16] *Juvenile Delinquency and Youth Crime,* Task Force Report (President's Commission on Law Enforcement and Administration of Justice, U. S. Government Printing Office, Washington, D.C., 1967), p. 223.

[17] Charles A. Reich, *The Greening of America* (New York. Bantam Books, 1971), p. 149.

[18] Kenneth Polk and Walter S. Schafer, "The Changing Concept of Education" in *School and Delinquency* (Englewood Cliffs, Prentice Hall, 1972), p. 7.

[19] *The Police,* Task Force Report (President's Commission on Law Enforcement and Administration of Justice, U.S. Government Printing Office, Washington, D.C., 1967), p. 1.

[20] *Ibid.,* p. 184.

rest quotas, toward certain racial and ethnic groups. Because of these preconceptions and prejudices and owing to "inadequate training, officers bring many juveniles before courts unnecessarily when other actions would have served better in particular cases." [21]

Although the police appear to have a good rating among the general public, other members of society, such as the blacks, have negative opinions of the effectiveness of the police.[22] Studies show that the black race is not alone in their feelings toward officers since many Latin Americans tend to "look upon the police as their enemies who protect only the white power structure." [23] In the case of many juveniles, the feeling toward the police is not much more encouraging. A good percentage of them believe that the "police accuse you of things you didn't do, (while an even greater percentage agree that) police try to act big shot and police try to get smart when you ask a question." [24]

Coupled with the aforementioned areas of delicate police relationships with society is the fact that juveniles would like the police to respect their autonomy, while the police desire respectful behavior from the youth. Many officers of the law simply do not realize that the autonomy and attitudes of the youths in question, especially those designated as being from the lower social and economic segments of society, have been a way of life for them which they are not about to give up in one meeting with law enforcement personnel. Here again is another perfect example of both officer and juvenile being caught up in the perpetual battle of *machismo,* and each others' view of what constitutes manhood.

The police make the smallest but thoroughly positive beginning toward alleviating the conditions mentioned when they begin to realize that "particularly with youth, it is important to use discretion in determining the differences between behavior which is dangerous enough to require action

---

[21] *Ibid.,* p. 96.

[22] *Ibid.,* p. 146.

[23] *Ibid.,* p. 149.

[24] *Ibid.,* p. 149.

and that which is not harmful, even though it may be different from the norm which adults hold for youth. Such behavior can be stifled only at the expense of creativity, liberty, and individual initiative. Delinquency prevention cannot be a cover for the undue enforcement of conformity." [25] However, the public must realize that Americans entrust the problem of crime to the police, "forgetting that they still operate with many of the limitations of constables of years past, even though today's citizens are no longer villagers." [26] The police cannot solve the inherent problems of schools that are not educating their young and parents who are failing in their primary task of raising children to be conscious not only of the law, but also of the rights of others.

Institutionalization—What Can Be Done to Change its Effect on Aggression

Institutionalization under its present form has failed the inmate as well as society itself. One federal district judge summed up the opinion of many professionals when he said, "I am persuaded that the institution of prison probably must end. In many respects it is as intolerable within the United States as was the institution of slavery, equally brutalizing to all involved, equally toxic to the social system, equally subversive to the brotherhood of man, more costly by some standards, and probably less rational." [27] Yet, the inmates are often viewed as the sole responsible agents for actions forced upon them, in part, by the physical as well as the psychological makeup of the prison itself. In spite of the fact that "somehow prisons do not belong to the social reality," [28] we know that "prisoners will continue to be con-

[25] Brademus, *op cit.*, p. E-6308.

[26] *The Police*, Task Force Report (President's Commission on Law Enforcement and Administration of Justice, U.S. Government Printing Office, Washington, D.C., 1967), p. 2.

[27] Jessica Mitford, *Kind and Unusual Punishment* (New York, Alfred A. Knopf, 1971), pp. 272-273. Remarks of Federal District Court Judge James Doyle of the Western District of Wisconsin in the *Morales v. Schmidt* case, ruling on the censorship of prison mail.

[28] John Gatlung, "Prison: The Organization of Dilemma" in Donald R.

fined in large groups under conditions of relative deprivation for some time to come, regardless of the consequences." [29] There can be no attempt at reform as long as
what Gillin said in his monumental work, *Taming the
Criminal*, in 1931, remains true today:

> What monuments to stupidity are these institutions we have
> built—stupidity not so much of the inmates as of free citizens!
> What a mockery of science are our prisons, the good and the bad
> together in one stupendous potpourri. How silly of us to think
> that we can prepare men for social life by reversing the ordinary
> processes of socialization—silence for the only animal with
> speech; repressive regimentation of men who are in prison
> because they need to learn how to exercise their activities in
> constructive ways; outward conformity to rules which repress all
> efforts at constructive expression . . . motivation by fear of
> punishment rather than hope of reward of appeal to their higher
> motives; rewards secured by the betrayal of a fellow rather than
> the development of a larger loyalty." [30]

The institutions' primary failure, relative to this study, is
simply that "the environment within the institution is an
infantile one where the individual is deprived of any kind
of identification that he is strong, masculine (or feminine),
worthwhile." [31]

Coupled with the deprivations imposed on the inmate by
the prison setting is the startling fact that 52 percent of the
American jail population at any given moment has not been
convicted of anything; they merely sit and await trial.[32]
They also become educated in the ways of more serious
crimes by those with whom they must share their quarters
or they are subjected to sexual assault by the more aggressive
inmates.

Cressey, *The Prison, Studies in Institutional Organization and Change* (New York, Holt Rinehart and Winston, 1961), p. 144.

[29] Gresham Sykes, *The Society of Captives* (Princeton, Princeton University Press, 1971), p. 132.

[30] John L. Gillin, "Taming the Criminal" (Montclair, N.J., Patterson, Smith, 1931), p. 51, quoted by Harry Elmer Barnes, "A Menace to Rehabitation" (*op. cit.*), p. 23.

[31] Linda Charlton, "The Terrifying Homosexual World of the Jail System," *New York Times,* April 25, 1971, p. 40.

[32] Conyers, *op. cit.*, p. 1104.

The real tragedy is that in spite of such findings by the National Advisory Committee on Criminal Justice Standards and Goals, that "many criminals should go free and many prisons should be replaced with programs more humane and effective than incarceration," [33] prisons and jails continue to be constructed as mere warehouses for inmates.

A primary element leading to sexual tension and aggression is the attitude of prison personnel toward sexuality in general. "Sexual attitudes in our society continue to be generally puritanical and such attitudes are carried into the punitative prison setting with even greater intensity." [34] In general "there seems to be an anxious concern among the staff about homosexual activity which is often expressed in a jocular, sarcastic, and sometimes hostile way." [35] Even the act of self-relief is not allowed, for "in prison . . . there is officially only a denial of sexuality, including in most institutions, regulations against masturbation . . . which (typifys) the broader denial of humanity." [36] According to Dr. Geis, the inmate suffering is two-fold, not only from institutional rules prohibiting masturbation, but also due to the fact that masturbation is often a source of concern for some men as well as youngsters who "retain superstitious thoughts relative to the dangers of masturbatory activities. The simplest approach and often the most effective means of dealing with this complaint in the prison setting is to educate the patient concerning masturbation, and barring psychotic over-concern or excessive guilt, to reassure him that under these circumstances masturbation may be the most desirable way to handle his sexual needs." [37]

In addition to changing prison rules relative to masturba-

---

[33] "U.S. Commission Says Many Criminals Should Go Free," *New York Times,* October 15, 1973, p. C-27.

[34] *A Handbook of Correctional Psychiatry,* Vol. 1 (Washington, D.C., U.S. Bureau of Prisons, Department of Justice, 1968), p. 15.

[35] *Ibid.*

[36] Charlton, *op. cit.* These remarks by Dr. Gilbert Geis professor of sociology at California State College of Los Angeles, California.

[37] *Handbook of Correctional Psychiatry,* Vol. 1 (Washington, D.C., U.S. Bureau of Prisons, Department of Justice, 1968), p. 14.

tion, prison personnel also have to change their sexual consciousness and awareness and put the welfare of the inmate above their own religious, educational, and social preferences. If masturbation can relieve sexual anxiety and therefore relieve sexual tension, then it should be allowed within the institution. Kinsey's statistics relative to this act among the general population are too well known to repeat here. However, they can serve to bolster the argument that men on the outside perform this act for sexual relief, why should it be denied the men within prison walls, be they teenager or adult.

Personal sexual liberation and understanding is not impossible and is much more easily accomplished when the staff of a correctional institution freely admits that they must get together as a body and discuss their own views relative to sexuality, if they are to render assistance to inmates in their care. Administrators of penal institutions, especially for young inmates, have the task of convincing the public as well as the legislature to support realistic programs aimed at sexual education within the institution itself. This is not an easy order, for public school systems often balk at frank courses with sexual information as their theme; however, administrators need only cite statistics relative to sexual assault in their institutions, as well as society in general, to gain some support for these necessary programs.

A vital suggestion is to include the security staff and the guards in on any sexual programs of this type. The correctional officers are closer to the inmate population than any other aspect of the institutional staff, be they educational, medical, or administrative. In this position it is important to realize that "probably the most important and strategically placed individuals involved in the problem of reconstruction of attitudes are the cell block officers and shop instructors— those representatives of the external community who are in direct, face-to-face daily contact with the inmate. How these individuals relate to the inmate determines, in the long run, not only the care and treatment policy of the institution, but that of the larger society as well." [38]

Classification [39] of inmates in reception and orientation centers should have been the rule more than a decade ago in penal institutions. Yet, they are still the exception in most institutions throughout the nation. Through classification, the sexually *different* or sexually attractive could be kept from mixing with the rest of the inmate population. This is not to condemn homosexuals or to inflict cruel and unusual punishment on anyone; rather it is intended to keep the weaker and often younger inmate apart from inmates with sexual desires that they will fulfill through assault. There is most assuredly abuse as well as the proper use of this type of classification and separation of inmates, but if proper and considerate programming is used, it can be successful.

In the 1950's one cell block at Soledad in California was called *queens' row*. Any known homosexual was transferred to this unit and though defined as nonpunitive, it was extremely so, since men confined in this wing were denied access to educational and vocational facilities as well as being served their meals segregated from the rest of the population. Also, the men worked primarily in the prison laundry segregated from the larger inmate population. This practice has since ceased, and many who show overt homosexual tendencies that cannot be controlled or lead to difficulties are sent to Vacaville, the hospital facility in the prison complex.[40] It appears that the Tombs, New York's Manhattan House of Detention, and the penal installation on Rikers Island both have lockups for men labeled as homosexuals. These types of jail-within-a-jail lockup may be a temporary answer toward protecting those in prison from sexual assault; however, it is

[38] Lloyd W. McCorkle and Richard Korn, "Resocialization Within the Walls," *The Annals of the American Academy of Political and Social Science,* 293:93 (May, 1954).

[39] Frank Loveland, "Classification in the Prison System" in *Contemporary Corrections,* Paul W. Tappan, ed. (New York, McGraw Hill, 1951), pp. 92-101.

[40] Peter C. Buffum, *Homosexuality in Prisons* (Washington, D.C., National Institute of Law Enforcement and Criminal Justice, U.S. Government Printing Office, February, 1972), p. 26.

a rather lugubrious remedy when one considers that, in most instances, heterosexually oriented males are the ones responsible for sexual attacks on other males.

Although the United States Prison Bureau appears to have no firm ruling on exactly what to do with overt homosexuals, any more than they appear to have rules pertaining to the sexual aggressor, they do attempt to address themselves to one aspect of the issue; the Bureau advocates that "the feminine appearing, sometime 'pretty' prisoner, must never be classified as a suspected homosexual . . . nor be issued identification that differentiates him from other prisoners. Such a classification may be harmful to him since he may begin to have doubts about his own masculinity. (Conversely), the jail officer should take care in deciding where to house the person who has a feminine appearance, as this prisoner has no defense against the aggressive homosexuals (and heterosexuals) found in jails and prisons. He must be housed away from them in a single cell if at all possible." [41] Again, the Bureau should also address itself to aggressive heterosexuals in order to approach the issue from its proper perspective.

Legal Approach to Sexual Aggression

We have seen that inmates will continue to be housed in prison-like settings for decades to come in spite of any movement to put an end to incarceration as it is now known. So, we are faced with doing something constructive *now* that will save the psychological, and in some instances, the physical lives of those inmates who cannot protect themselves from the jockers and wolves that prowl the halls of training schools, prisons and jails.

The courts have finally become aware of the amount of sexual aggression occurring in penal institutions. In 1970, in the case of *Holt v. Sarver*, the courts found that the inmate who is physically attractive to the other men frequently is raped in the "barracks and no one will come to his aid, while

---

[41] *The Jail Its Operation and Management*, Nick Papas, ed. (Washington, D.C., U.S. Bureau of Prisons and University Wisconsin, February, 1972), p. 26. (parentheses mine)

the trustees will look on with indifference or satisfaction. Some of the inmates are put in such fear that they will come to the front of the barracks and cling to the bars at night." [42] From realizations such as these there has come a faint awareness that the prisoner has a right to expect protection while he is confined. At the least, the courts have recognized, in the case of the *United States v. Muniz*,[43] the right of the prisoner to enter civil suits in federal prisons where one inmate is attacked by another. The court has determined that prison officials must exercise ordinary care for prisoners' protection and safety. If they fail to meet this standard, they are liable for damages when one inmate is physically or sexually assaulted by another. This decision may result in lax and callous correctional officials being indicted for their many and obvious failures to provide adequate protection for all the inmates in their care.

These cases and court decisions are not an immediate lifesaver to the victims of aggression in our institutions at present. However, cases such as these are beginning to set precedents in our penal institutions. The guards as well as the administrators are personally responsible for abuses suffered by weaker inmates at the hands of aggressors. No longer are prison officials given *carte blanche* to run the prison their way. As late as 1971 District Judge Zirpoli rejected the idea that a "state prisoner is committed to the custody of the Department Of Corrections and as such may be confined in any manner chosen by the Director, subject only to statutory guidelines and the protection of the 'cruel and unusual punishment' clause of the eighth amendment." [44]

In *Hamilton v. Schiro* the court held that confinement under conditions of overcrowding, deteriorating buildings,

---

[42] "Sexual Assaults and Forced Homosexual Relations in Prison: Cruel and Unusual Punishment," *Albany Law Review*, 32:432 (1972).

[43] *Federal Tort Claims Act*, 28, U.S.C. 1346. See *United States v. Muniz*, 374 U.S. 150, 1963. The applicable standard is stated under 18 U.S.C. 4042 which provides that prison officials must exercise ordinary care for safety and protection of prisoners.

[44] *Clutchette v. Procunier*, F. Supp. (N.D. Cal., June 21, 1971) as cited in Buffum, *op. cit.*, pp. 32-33.

unsanitary conditions, inadequate guards, inadequate medical facilities, and sexual assault violated the rights of the inmates under the eighth amendment.[45] The courts, in these decisions, are no longer blaming the inmates *in toto* for *perverse acts* committed among themselves; rather they are recognizing that institutionalization itself has something to do with bringing the inherent actions of aggressive individuals to the surface at the expense of the weaker inmates.

Conjugal Visits—Solution or Further Problem

There has been some speculation and attempt at implementation within the field of corrections to allow conjugal visits within prisons for those men who are married. In 1967 conjugal visits were hailed in the Mississippi state penitentiary system as probably responsible for saving marriages as well as reducing recidivism and homosexuality.[46] Originally, the "prison allowed inmates to bring girl friends and wives into the prisoners' regular sleeping quarters. The prisoners were allowed to hang blankets around their beds for privacy. Later the institution allowed inmates to build separate units—and girl friends were barred." [47] It is interesting to note that the "wigwam," or "chuckwagon," or "hunks," names given to the forms made by the blankets being placed around a bed for privacy during these heterosexual activities, are the same practices utilized by those jockers and wolves when they force a weaker inmate to have sex with them.

This privilege appears to have led to further problems within the institution where it was granted. Girl friends were admitted at the outset of the program but were later prevented from participating further. In most instances those men who cannot share the same privileges resent those who can benefit from such a plan. A prominent criminologist

---

[45] "Sexual Assaults and Forced Homosexual Relations in Prison: Cruel and Unusual Punishment," *Albany Law Review*, 32:431 (1972).

[46] "Conjugal Visits In Prison Hailed," *New York Times*, August 15, 1967, p. 26.

[47] *Ibid.*

found that even those who participate in such a program find that conjugal visits are "just too blatant for most people to accept." [48] Ex-prisoners who were given the privilege felt that "you're dehumanizing the wife along with the husband or vice versa," [49] in such visits. The furlough program, discussed later, appears to be a more socially acceptable solution to the need for visitation of inmates with their loved ones.

Can Consenting Homosexual Acts in Prison Be Legal? Would It Help the Problem of Sexual Deprivation?

There appears to be an 'immediate' solution to the phenomena of consenting homosexuality in prison. In the case of *Griswold v. Connecticut,* the state's birth control law was ruled unconstitutional. While the case "deals with the limited fact of marital privacy, its reasoning is sufficiently broad to encompass many varied situations. That is, *Griswold* opens the doors for further development of a protection to personal conduct and thought. . . . The *Griswold* notion of privacy will likely have an impact on the legality of miscegenation statutes . . . loyalty oaths, (and) homosexuality." [50]

Evidently one noted sociologist feels the case may have an impact within penal institutions. Buffum states that "the reasons for not prosecuting consensual homosexual acts, whether in a prison setting or otherwise, seem persuasive. In addition a constitutional argument can be made that consensual sexual activity between adults is protected by the constitutional right to privacy." [51] as noted in the *Griswold* ruling. "Those cases upholding the right of privacy in this area should be considered in the prison context as well." [52]

There is no need to feel that correctional institutions would become comparable to Sodom and Gomorrah. What is needed is a realistic approach to what is already happening

---

[48] Charlton, *op. cit.,* p. 40.
[49] *Ibid.*
[50] *Northwestern University Law Review,* 6:828-829 (January-February, 1966).
[51] Buffum, *op. cit.,* p. 33.
[52] *Ibid.*

in prisons and jails at the present time. Conjugal visits cannot possibly alleviate the sexual urges and desires of men who
cannot participate in such a program. It is time to stop the
child-like attitudes of prohibiting every form of sexual expression for the inmates, from masturbation to sexual expression with a fellow inmate, if it is on a consensual basis. If
there are inmates who have sexual desires for other inmates,
who feel about them in a like manner, then it is within the
realm of possibility for the institutions to make accommoda-
tion for this type of activity. As we have seen, sex is being conducted while the administrators and guards turn their backs
and even laugh while an inmate is raped. Is it so implausible
for these same administrators and guards to now control the
sexual activity in a productive manner? Evidentally one
author feels that it is possible to have such relationships occurring since he notes that in "some jails and prisons (such
as the Tombs in New York and the lockups on Rikers Island)
such men (homosexuals) are frequently isolated, allowing
them to gain with impunity such erotic pleasure as they may
find with each other." [53] Although this attitude appears to
be slightly condescending, it does appear to allow for sexual
relations among those inmates who desire one another without causing further hardship with the custodial staff.

Evidently there is an avenue open to relieve sexual pressures among men who are consenting parties to sexual acts.
It is time that correctional institutions, as well as society
itself, find the social, legal, and educational elasticity not only
to allow such relations to occur, but also lend some structural
and directive procedures to insure its *normalcy*.

Photographs and Magazines—A Help or Hindrance to Sexual Expression

As rules are now written in most jails and prisons, the inmate is allowed to have only a few pictures; some institutions

---

[53] Edward Sagarin, and Donal E. J. MacNamara, *The Homosexual as a Crime Victim*. A paper presented at the First International Symposium on Victimology, Hebrew University, Jerusalem, Israel, September 2nd-6th, 1973, p. 38.

allow only one [54] in his cell, and these must be of his family or loved ones. This ruling leads to the formation of an underground where contraband, in the form of pornography, becomes the medium of exchange. Men will sell cigarettes, candy, and even their bodies for pictures that are available to high school teenagers from street corner newsstands. It is both a dubious and specious argument to prevent such magazines as *Playboy* from being read in the correctional centers. We have seen that hundreds of rape reports have been documented in institutions where such material is strictly forbidden. It may well be time to attempt a lengthy experiment and allow certain 'manly' books within the walls and assess their affects. They might alter the present state of affairs wherein one coveted picture can lead to aggression and even murder among confined men.

Further Suggestions

One of the first and certainly feasible prohibitions that should go out to all prisons and jails is the order to cease all forms of experimentation on inmates, be it medical, psychological, or pharmaceutical. No inmate has the freedom to give his mind or body voluntarily for such experimentation. In a penal setting experimentation is simple exploitation of the victim, and that is what the inmate is—a victim. In turn, experimentation programs establish other satellite worlds within the correctional setting. Those with the financial rewards gained from such a program can and do easily assume the role of the aggressor in sexual exploitation of those inmates who do not have equal opportunities to participate in such a program. Even if sexual exploitation were not involved in such programs, "testimony before the Health Subcommittee has revealed that in the coercive atmosphere of a prison, inmates are more than willing to submit to drug experiments and other experimental programs in order to secure money or change of location and conditions or to

---

[54] Personal observation of the author while Educational Director at the Whalley Avenue Correctional Center (Jail), New Haven, Connecticut.

please the parole board by a record showing cooperation with the prison authority." [55]

Another suggestion to relieve tension and sexual exploitation is the immediate reversal of the philosophy wherein "the principle of rehabilitation is being served simultaneously with the principles of prevention of crime. One wonders, therefore, if under present circumstances . . . the principles are not in essence contradictory." [56] According to available evidence, "the foremost responsibilities assigned to prison officials are maintenance of custodial security and protection of society against convicted offenders." [57] There simply must be a reversal of those statistics that indicate that only one person in twenty within penal institutions has anything to do with treatment, while the others perform services that are largely custodial in nature." [58] Even more tragic is the fact that it appears that "chaplains, caseworkers, physicians . . . either share the repressive orientation of the custodial staff or are relatively isolated and uninfluential," [59] in their assigned missions relative to the inmates.

The historical training given to guards needs to be altered radically. Each correctional officer is told to be firm, fair, but never friendly or informal to inmates. Yet, it appears that "if policies of nonfraternization (of guards with inmates) were relaxed, in combination with increased staff training in human relations, then the line officer might serve to reduce prison homosexuality by providing one outlet for inmate affectual needs." [60]

Community Corrections

There is a slow but growing trend toward community correctional facilities and "the emerging model for dealing

[55] Senator Sam J. Ervin, Jr., "Federal Funding for Behavior Modification," *Congressional Record* (Senate), vol. 119, no. 69, May 8, 1973, p. 8517.

[56] Szabo, *op. cit.*, p. 72.

[57] Cressey, *op. cit.*, p. 331.

[58] Mangel, *op. cit.*, p. 53.

[59] *Corrections*, Task Force Report (The President's Commission on Law Enforcement and Administration of Justice, U.S. Government Printing Office, Washington, D.C., 1967), p. 47.

[60] Buffum, *op. cit.*, p. 30.

with offenders will feature many shades of community-based placement for both juveniles and adults. Total institutions segregated from the community may be necessary for a small percentage of dangerous people housing a much smaller proportion of the total offender population than that which is now kept under constant lock and key." [61] It has been found that in excess of 70 percent of all inmates could be placed in community-based correctional facilities almost immediately. Another 15 per cent may be in need of short-term community oriented confinement. The remaining 15 percent requiring longer confinement should be treated with eventual hopes for a return to society and a normal community life.[62] The whole emphasis upon this approach to corrections is on "returning to the community its responsibility for dealing with behavior it defines as anti-social or deviant." [63]

Women in Corrections, How they Can Affect Sexual Aggression

Prisons and jails have been traditionally the domain of men since male offenders far outnumber females; the personnel in these institutions have largely been limited to men, except for a few secretarial and office positions. Women should be hired as teachers, counselors, and paraprofessionals in order to make the prison atmosphere as similar to the outside world as possible. With proper supervision and planning for classrooms and counseling areas, the constant concern for security can be assured to these new arrivals to the field of corrections.[64] Women functioning in this manner "would keep inmates in contact, although in a limited way,

---

[61] Milton Burdman, "Realism in Community Based Correctional Services," *Annals Of American Academy Of Political and Social Science*, 383:71 (January, 1969).

[62] *Ibid.*

[63] Eleanor Harlow, J. Robert Weber, and Leslie T. Wilkins, "Community Based Correctional Programs, Models and Practices," (National Institute of Mental Health for The Studies Of Crime and Delinquency, Rockville, 1967), p. 33.

[64] Dr. Anthony M. Scacco, Jr., "Some Observations About Women and Their Role in the Field of Corrections," *American Journal Of Corrections*, 34:9-12 (March-April, 1972).

with the real life situation composed of both men and women."⁶⁵

Much to the chagrin of the public is the new attempt for correctional institutions to go coed. Connecticut began such a program for its adjudicated juvenile offenders in 1973 when the Connecticut School for Boys merged with the Long Lane School for Girls. Although too early to assess the success of the program, to date no serious incidents appear to have marred the experiment. The Connecticut Prison, scheduled to open in 1976, will accommodate both male and female adults as well as youthful offenders. Housing shall be separate for each group, but there will be an integration of the sexes in classrooms and other educational and reform situations. Dr. Elizabeth Flynn of the Clearinghouse for Criminal Justice Planning and Architecture of the University of Illinois says that this type of coed institutionalization works as a defusing situation and there is an entirely different atmosphere in such an integrated setting.⁶⁶

New York recently suffered a blow to a similar coeducational correctional endeavor, which reflects the punitive philosophy that the public retains toward those in prison. The unique educational correctional reform measure was to provide prisoners with an opportunity to attend their own college, aimed at preparing them for a two year liberal arts or science degree. However, the "plan, regrettably has proven too sensible and too humane for the Legislature, which is trying to kill it by eliminating a projected $500,000 appropriation from Governor Wilson's budget . . . The real reason for the negative response to this sound idea is not its cost . . . Rather, the concept has fallen victim to the vindictive notion that any constructive effort at rehabilitation represents a coddling of criminals."⁶⁷ Evidently, it is still somewhat fashionable to believe that the "judge pronounces sentence

---

⁶⁵ *Ibid.*, p. 12.

⁶⁶ "Connecticut Is Going Co-Ed," *New York Times*, May 27, 1973, p. E-10.

⁶⁷ "The Difficult Struggle to Achieve Prison Reform in New York," *New York Times*, March 23, 1974, p. 30.

and the public feels that justice is done. They seem to forget altogether that life goes on in prison and beyond." [68]

Furloughs are Feasible and Return a Sense of Normalcy to the Inmate Even in His Sexual Outlook

There is great need to utilize the furlough system in corrections. Men with records showing good behavior should be released for weekends at home with their families and relatives. States such as Massachusetts have received negative publicity regarding its release of inmates for weekend leaves; unfortunately, proponents of a get tough attitude have attempted to use a few negative results of this experimental program to nullify all attempts of other states to attempt similar programs. Yet, Connecticut has reported overwhelming success in its furlough programs. Of the 2,993 furloughs granted during the period of March 1, 1971 to February 7, 1972, there were only eleven cases where inmates were arrested while on leave, and in only one instance was it necessary for the police to apprehend an inmate who committed a felony.[69] Many of the adults, as well as youthful offenders who are also included in this program, listed a desire to be with family, wives and girl friends,[70] as important reasons why they desired a furlough and why they made certain their behavior measured up to the required norms for being granted leave from the institution. In this sense, released time from the correctional setting helped in maintaining normal sexual relationships concerning these men and those close to them on the outside.

The Courts—Their Actions Affect the Inmate Population and Therefore the Opportunity for Acts of Aggression

Perhaps the area in need of the most drastic and creative action, relative to the offender, is that of the criminal

---

[68] Mattick, *op. cit.*, p. 6.

[69] Dr. Anthony M. Scacco, Jr., "Connecticut's Furlough Program," *Congressional Record*, Vol. 119, No. 76, May 21, 1973, p. E-3322.

[70] *Ibid.*

courts.[71] The public views the courtroom as the bastion of our legal system where the guilty are punished and the innocent most certainly are vindicated. Yet, the "dignity of the courtroom, the respectable front for the sordid practice of the criminal justice system, strikes many observers as particularly offensive." [72] In all too many instances poor whites, Puerto Ricans, and blacks are discriminated against in court procedures when the victims receive sentences because of their inability to post bail or pay fines.[73] All too often "the criminal trial has the function of public edification rather than that of the welfare of the individual wrong-doers who pass over its stage in endless procession. In fixed formula and procedure the trial reiterates the moral parables of our child-rearing and, in the person of the judge, brings to the transgressor a power and punitive enforcement once exercised by the parent." [74]

Immediate reforms within the criminal justice system should encompass speedier trials for misdemeanors; a tightening of sentencing laws to make them more consistent and punishment less disparate; elimination of sentences calling for payment of fines or in the alternative, incarceration for those who cannot pay; the decriminalization of victimless crimes; the prohibition of prosecutorial coercive inducements to entering a plea of guilty, and the banning of any plea negotiations without the presence of defense counsel.

The entire parole system and concept needs to be reorganized, for presently they are too oppressive in most states to be effective deterrents to further criminal acts by the parolee. Further, a revised concept of probation is needed since it has been shown that 60 to 70 percent of court adjudications for adult offenders could be placed on immediate probation and the percentage would almost certainly be

[71] *Yale Review Of Law and Social Action,* vol. 2, no. 1 (New Haven Connecticut, Yale Law School, Fall, 1971), p. 20.

[72] *Ibid.*

[73] *Ibid.*

[74] American Friends Service Committee, *Struggle for Justice:* A Report on Crime and Punishment in America (New York, Hill and Wang, 1971), p. 60.

higher with juvenile offenders. New York's parole system has been called "oppressive and arbitrary, a tragic failure beyond reform." [75] Thus, there is no secret that, functioning properly, this one aspect of the judicial system could keep many men out of institutions and therefore away from the possibility of becoming a victim of sexual attack.

Within the institutions the inmates should be allowed an official inmate bill of rights, access to the media, attorneys' rights when charged with a crime within the walls, and the right to counsel in preparing briefs for their parole. Pretrial intervention is desperately needed whereby, after arrest but prior to trial, conviction, and sentencing, a youthful offender could be given a ninety-day suspended sentence to determine his ability to function in the community rather than being locked in a jail or prison where sexual attack is almost a guarantee. During this time the offender would be given counseling and assistance, and upon successful completion of the program, charges would be dismissed thereby avoiding institutionalization as well as a criminal record.

Work release programs where the offender is confined in the institution only at night or on weekends needs to be more broadly implemented. This method gives the offender his dignity while simultaneously providing for supervision by the penal institution and most importantly does not completely disrupt the normal family and social ties of the offender.

All of the aforementioned suggestions depend upon a change of attitude on the part of the public, the police, correctional personnel and the courts as well. H. L. Menkin in commenting about Havelock Ellis as "undoubtedly the most diligent and scientific student of the sex problem that the world has yet seen," [76] says that "the trouble with Ellis is that he tells the truth which is the unsafest of all things to tell. His crime is that he is a man who prefers facts to

---

[75] Tom Goldstein, "Parole System Scored in State (N.Y.) It is Called 'Oppressive' and Arbitrary By Panel," New York *Times,* March 6, 1974, p. C-15.

[76] H. L. Mencken, "On Being an American," in James T. Farrell, ed., *Prejudices: A Selection* (New York, Vintage, 1958), pp. 88-89.

illusions, and knows what he is talking about. Such men are never popular. The public taste is for merchandise of a precisely opposite character. The way to please is to proclaim in a confident manner, not what is true, but what is merely comforting." [77]

This endeavor has been to proclaim what is true; as for comfort, that may well be impossible in the face of the facts presented herein.

---

[77] *Ibid.*

BIBLIOGRAPHY

BOOKS

Amemiya, Eiji C.: The delinquent sub-culture: Population and projections. In Graubard, Paul: *Children Against Schools*. Chicago, Follett Educational Corporation, 1969.

Barnes, Harry Elmer: "A menace to rehabilitation." *The Future of Imprisonment in a Free Society*, Chicago, St. Leonard House, 1965.

Barry, Leonard: *Prison Interviews*. In Shalleck, Jamie (Ed.). New York, Grossman, 1972.

Carmichael, Stokely, and Hamilton, Charles: *Black Power, The Politics of Liberation in America*. New York, Vintage, 1967.

Clark, Kenneth B.: *Dark Ghetto*, New York, Harper and Row, 1965.

Clark, Ramsey: *Crime in America*. New York, Pocket Books, 1971.

Cressey, Donald: *The Prison, Studies in Institutional Organization and Change*. New York, Holt, Rinehart and Winston, 1961.

Cressey, Donald and Ward, David A.: *Delinquency, Crime and the Social Process*. New York, Harper and Row, 1969.

Ellis, Albert, and Abarbanel, Albert: *The Encyclopedia of Sexual Behavior*. New York, Hawthorn Books, 1967.

Ellis, Havlock: Studies in the Psychology of Sex. In Ellis, Albert and Abarbanel, Albert (Eds.): *The Encyclopedia of Sexual Behavior*. New York, Hawthorne Books, 1967.

Empey, La Mar T.: *Studies in Delinquency Alternatives to Incarceration*. Washington, D.C., U.S. Department of Health, Education and Welfare, 1967.

Galtung, John: Prison, the organization of dilemma. *The Prison Studies In Institutional Organization and Change*, New York, Holt, Rinehart and Winston, 1961.

Goffman, Erving: *Asylums*. New York, Doubleday, 1961.

Graubard, Paul: *Children Against Schools*. Chicago, Follett Educational, 1969.

Grimshaw, Allen D.: *Racial Violence in the United States*. Chicago, Aldine Publishing, 1969.

Griswold, Jack, Misenheimer, Mike, and Powers, Art: *An Eye For An Eye*. New York, Holt, Rinehart and Winston, 1970.

Harrington, Michael: The American character. *The Center For Study Of Democratic Institutions*, Santa Barbara, Fund For The Republic, 1972.

117

Irwin, John: *The Felon.* Englewood, Prentice Hall, 1970.

Jones, Le Roi: *What Does Non-Violence Mean? Law Resistance American Attitudes Toward Authority.* In Veysey, Lawrence (Ed.). New York, Harper Torch, 1971.

Karlen, Arno: *Sexuality and Homosexuality, a New View.* New York, W. W. Norton, 1971.

Kinsey, Alfred C., Pomeroy, Wardell B., and Martin, Clyde E.: *Sexual Behavior in the Human Male.* Philadelphia, W. B. Saunders, 1948.

Laite, William: *The United States vs William Laite.* Washington, D.C., Acropolis, 1972.

Loveland, Frank: Classification in the prison system. In Tappan, Paul W. (Ed.): *Contemporary Corrections.* New York, McGraw Hill, 1951.

Mattick, Hans W.: A discussion of the issue. *The Future Of Imprisonment In A Free Society,* vol. 2, Chicago, St. Leonard House, 1965.

May, Rollo: *Power and Innocence, A Search for the Sources of Violence.* New York, W. W. Norton, 1972.

Mencken, H. L.: *Prejudices, A Selection.* New York, Vintage, 1958.

Menninger, Karl: *The Crime of Punishment.* New York, Viking Press, 1968.

Millett, Kate: *Sexual Politics.* New York, Avon, 1970.

Mitford, Jessica: *Kind and Unusual Punishment—The Prison Business.* New York, Alfred A. Knopf, 1973.

Ollendorff, Robert H. V.: *The Juvenile Homosexual Experience And Its Effect on Adult Sexuality.* New York, Julian Press, 1966.

Polk, Kenneth, and Schafer, Walter S.: The changing concept of education. *School and Delinquency.* Englewood Cliffs, Prentice Hall, 1972.

Reich, Charles A.: *The Greening Of America.* New York, Bantam, 1971.

Reiss, Albert J.: The social integration of queers and peers. In Cressey, Donald R. and Ward, David A. (Eds.): *Delinquency Crime and the Social Process.* New York, Harper and Row, 1969.

Reiss, Ira L.: *Studies In Human Sexual Behavior: The American Scene.* In Shiloh, Ailon (Ed.). Springfield, Thomas, 1970.

Robinson, Patricia, Poor black women, A collective statement. In Rozack, Theodore, and Rozack, Betty (Eds.): *Masculine and Feminine Readings in Sexual Mythology and Liberation of Women.* New York, Harper and Row, 1969.

Short, James F., and Nye, Ivan F.: Extent of unrecorded juvenile delinquency, tentative conclusions. In Teele, James E. (Ed.): *Juvenile Delinquency, A Reader.* Itasca, F. E. Peacock, 1970.

Silberman, Charles, E.: *Crisis in Black and White.* New York, Random House, 1964.

Silberman, Charles E.: *Crisis in The Classroom—The Remaking Of American Education.* New York, Vintage Books, 1971.

Struggle for Justice, A Report on Crime and Punishment in America, American Friends Service Committee. New York, Hill and Wang, 1971.

Sykes, Ghresham: *The Society Of Captives.* Princeton, Princeton University Press, 1971.

Tiger, Lionel: *Men In Groups.* New York, Vintage, 1971.

Toch, Hans: *Violent Men an Inquiry Into the Psychology of Violence.* Chicago, Aldine, 1969.

X, Malcom: *The Autobiography of Malcom X.* New York, Grove Press, 1966.

ARTICLES

Alberts, Lawrence, and De Riemer, Thomas A.: Connecticut watchdogs human research experiments. *American Journal of Correction,* vol. 35, no. 2, 1973.

Bayh, Birch: Toward juvenile justice. *American Scholar,* vol. 40, no. 4, Autumn, 1971.

Block, Herbert A.: Social Pressures of Confinement Toward Sexual Deviation. *Journal of Social Therapy,* vol. 6, 1960.

Burdman, Milton: Realism in community based correctional services. *Annals of the American Academy of Political and Social Science,* vol. 381, 1969.

Clended, Richard J.: What's the matter with corrections. *Federal Probation,* vol. 35, no. 3, 1971.

Cloward, Richard: Social control in prisons. *Social Science Research Council,* Pamphlet No. 15, March, 1960.

Davis, Alan J.: Sexual assaults in the Philadelphia prison system and sheriff's vans. *Trans-Action,* vol. 6, no. 2, December, 1968.

Divans, Kenneth, and West, Larry M.: Prison or slavery. *The Black Scholar,* vol. 3, no. 2, 1971.

Gagnon, John H., and William, Simon: The social meaning of prison homosexuality. *Federal Probation,* vol. 32, no. 1, 1968.

Garofalo, Ralph: Portrait of a rapist. *Newsweek Magazine,* vol. LXXXII, August 20, 1973.

Gibbons, Don. C.: Violence in American society the challenge to corrections. *The American Journal of Corrections,* vol. 31, no. 2, March-April, 1969.

Horrock, Nicholas: The new breed of convict, black, angry, and radical. *Newsweek Feature Service,* vol. 23, September, 1971.

Huffman, Arthur V.: Sex deprivation in a prison community. *Journal of Social Therapy,* vol. 6, no. 4, 1964.

Kassebaum, Gene: Sex in prison. *Sexual Behavior,* vol. 2, no. 1, Leonard Gross, editor, New York, Interpersonal Publications, January, 1972.

Lyston, Herry L.: Stress in correctional institutions. *Journal of Social Therapy,* vol. 6, 1960.

McCorkle, Lloyd W., and Korn, Richard: Resocialization within the walls. *Annals of American Academy of Political and Social Science,* vol. 293, May, 1954.

Mangel, Charles: How to make a criminal out of a child. *Look magazine,* vol. 35, no. 13, June 29, 1971.

Mills, James: I have nothing to do with justice. *Life Magazine,* vol. 70, no. 9, March 12, 1972.

Mitford, Jessica: Experiments behind bars. *The Atlantic Magazine,* vol. 321, no. 1, January, 1973.

Ross, Sid and Kupferberg, Herbert, "A Waste of Lives—And Your Money, The Shame Of Our County Jails," *Parade Magazine,* November 4, 1973.

Roth, Lauren: Territoriality and homosexuality in a male prison. *American Journal of Orthopsychiatry,* vol. 41, no. 3, 1971.

Scacco, Anthony M., Jr.: Some observations about women and their role in the field of corrections. *American Journal of Correction,* vol. 34, no. 2, 1972.

Scudder, Kenyon J.: The open institution. *Annals of American Political and Social Science,* vol. 239, May, 1954.

"Sexual Assaults and Forced Homosexual Relationships in Prison: Cruel and Unusual Punishment," *Albany Law Journal,* vol. 32, no. 2, 1972.

Tannenbaum, Frank: The professional criminal. *The Century,* vol. 110, May-October, 1925.

Wallace, Michael: The uses of violence in American history. *American Scholar,* vol. 40, no. 1, Winter, 1971.

LAW REVIEWS

Northwestern University Law Review, vol. 6, no. 6, Chicago, Illinois, Northwestern University School of Law, January-February, 1966.

Yale Review of Law and Social Action, vol. 2, no. 1, New Haven, Connecticut, Yale Law School, Fall, 1971.

Ward, Jack, L.: Homosexual behavior of the institutionalized delinquent. *Psychiatric Quarterly Supplement,* vol. 32, 1958.

Wheeler, Stanton: Socialization in correctional institutions. *Crime and Justice,* edited by Leon Radzinowicz and Marvin Wolfgang, vol. 3, New York, Basic Books, 1971.

Wiggins, Frederick: The truth about Attica by an inmate. *National Review,* vol. 24, no. 12, March 31, 1972.

Zabo, Denis: Do prisons have a future. *The Future of Imprisonment in a Free Society,* vol. 2, Chicago, St. Leonard House, 1965.

TASK FORCE REPORTS

Corrections, Task Force Report, President's Commission on Law Enforcement and Administration of Justice, Washington, D.C., United States Government Printing Office, 1967.

The Courts, Task Force Report, President's Commission on Law Enforcement and Administration of Justice, Washington, D.C., United States Government Printing Office, 1967.

Juvenile Delinquency, Task Force Report, President's Commission on Law Enforcement and Administration of Justice, Washington, D.C., United States Government Printing Office, 1967.

The Police, Task Force Report, President's Commission on Law Enforcement and Administration of Justice, Washington, D.C., United States Government Printing Office, 1967.

NEWSPAPERS

Brademus, John, "Head Start Success or Failure," *Congressional Record,* October 4, 1973.

Charlton, Linda, "The Terrifying Homosexual World of the Jail System," *New York Times,* April 25, 1971.

"Children's Justice Called A Failure by Judicial Panel," New York *Times,* October 29, 1973.

Clinton, Arthur, "The Half Outs," *New York Daily News,* December 16, 1971.

"Conjugal Visits Hailed in Prison," *New York Times,* August 15, 1967.

"Connecticut Is Going Co-Ed," *New York Times,* May 27, 1973.

Conyers, John Jr., "The Criminal Justice System," *Congressional Record,* February 22, 1973.

"The Difficult Struggle to Achieve Prison Reform," New York *Times,* March 23, 1974.

Ervin, Sam, Jr., "Federal Funding for Behavior Modification," *Congressional Record,* May 8, 1973.

Goldstein, Tom, "Parole System Scored In State" (New York), New York *Times,* March 6, 1974.

Kihss, Peter, "Boys Home Depicted as Base for Criminal Raids," New York *Times,* December 14, 1973.

"Massachusetts Reform to Doom Youth Prisons," New York *Times,* January 31, 1972.

Moore, Winston E., "A Human Approach to Prison Reform," *Congressional Record,* January 11, 1973.

Morgan, Ted, "Entombed," *New York Times Magazine,* February 17, 1974.

Rader, Doston, "The Sexual Nature of Violence," New York *Times,* October 22, 1973.

Railsback, Tom, "Juveniles in Jail," *Congressional Record,* September 25, 1973.

Scacco, Anthony M., Jr., "Connecticut's Furlough Program," *Congressional Record,* May 27, 1973.

"U.S. Commission Says Many Criminals Should Go Free," *New York Times,* October 15, 1973.

UNPUBLISHED PAPERS

Bartollas, Clemens and Miller, Stuart J. "The White Victim in a Black Society. A paper presented at the Annual Meeting of The American Society of Criminology, November 2-6, 1973.

Denfeld, Duane and Hopkins, Andrew. "Racial-Ethnic Identification in Prisons, Right On From The Inside." A paper presented to The Eastern Sociological Meeting, Boston, April, 1972.

Dintz, Simon, Miller, Stuart J., and Bartollas, Clemens. "Inmate Exploitation—A Study on the Juvenile Victim." A paper presented at the First International Symposium on Victimology, Hebrew University, September 2-6, 1973.

Jordan, Daniel and Dye, Larry L. "Delinquency an Assessment of the Juvenile Delinquency and Control Act of 1968." Unpublished paper. University Massachusetts School of Education, 1970.

Sagarin, Edward and MacNamara, Donal. "The Homosexual as a Crime Victim." A paper presented at the First International Symposium on Victimology, Hebrew University, September 2-6, 1973.

BOOKLETS AND PAMPHLETS

Buffum, Peter C., *Homosexuality In Prisons.* Washington, D.C., United States Government Printing Office, February, 1972.

Harlow, Eleanor, Weber, Robert J, and Wilkins, Leslie T., *Community Based Correctional Programs, Models and Practices.* Rockville, Maryland, National Institute of Mental Health, For The Studies Of Crime and Delinquency, 1967.

Papas, Nick, *The Jail: Its Operation and Management.* Washington, D.C., U.S. Bureau Of Prisons in cooperation with The University Of Wisconsin Extension Services, 1973.

Sykes, Gresham, and Messinger, Sheldon L., *The Inmate Social Code And Its Functions.* New York, Social Science Research Council, Pamphlet No. 15, 1960.

AUTHOR INDEX

SUBJECT INDEX

A

Attica, 43

B

Black
aggressor, 62, 63, 64, 71, 73, 74, 75
bitterness, 90, 91
homosexuals, 61
masculinity assertion, 84, 85
role reversal
minority and majority, 5
traditional discriminations, 90, 91
use of middleclass values with inmates, 74, 75
women
see Women
Bound-overs,
definition of, 59

C

Cagemen,
definition of, 12
Chuckwagon, 106
Cloacal regions, 7
Coed correctional institutions, 111, 112
Community,
corrections in, 110, 111,
Connecticut,
Prison, 112
Reformatory, 25, 26, 27, 28, 39, 40, 41, 60
School for Boys, 11, 48, 49, 50, 51, 112
Training School in, 61
Conjugal visits, 106
Cottage,
definition of, 41
Crime Prevention,
education and socialization, 94
police role, 97, 98
school role, 95, 96

Criminal courts, 114, 115, 116

D

Detention centers, 14
Dress codes, 23, 24, 25
Drugs,
experiments with, 28

E

Emasculation, 76
Experimentation,
on inmates, 109, 110

F

Fairfield County Jail, 20
Female,
assault, 82
Furloughs, 113

G

Griswold vs. Connecticut, 107

H

Health Subcommittee, 109
Herrschaft, 80
see also Max Weber
Heterosexually oriented males, 4
Holmesberg Prison, 19, 20
Homosexual acts in prison,
as solution for sexual deprivation, 107
Homosexuals, 4, 10, 35, 54, 61
classification in institutions, 103
queens' row, 103
United States Prison Bureau, 104
Hunks,
definition of, 106

I

Individuality,
development of for juveniles, 36

125